WELCOMING THE NATIONS

INTERNATIONAL VOICES IN BIBLICAL STUDIES

Editor
Jione Havea

Editorial Board
Jin Young Choi
Emily Colgan
Musa Dube
Julián Andrés González
David Joy
Gerald O. West

Number 13

WELCOMING THE NATIONS: INTERNATIONAL SOCIORHETORICAL EXPLORATIONS

Edited by
Vernon K. Robbins and Roy R. Jeal

SBL PRESS

Atlanta

Copyright © 2020 by SBL Press

All rights reserved. No part of this work may be reproduced or transmitted in any form or by any means, electronic or mechanical, including photocopying and recording, or by means of any information storage or retrieval system, except as may be expressly permitted by the 1976 Copyright Act or in writing from the publisher. Requests for permission should be addressed in writing to the Rights and Permissions Office, SBL Press, 825 Houston Mill Road, Atlanta, GA 30329 USA.

Library of Congress Control Number: 2020947824

Contents

Acknowledgments..vii
Abbreviations...ix

Introduction
    Vernon K. Robbins and Roy R. Jeal..1

    Part 1: Development and Emergence of International Sociorhetorical
              Interpretation

Retrospect and Prospect of Sociorhetorical Interpretation
    Duane F. Watson..11

From Otago, Africa, and India to Asia, Australia, and Oceania
    Vernon K. Robbins..19

Strengths and Gaps of Foundations for Sociorhetorical Exploration
    Shively T. J. Smith...33

    Part 2: Explorations in Australia and Oceania

An Australian Ecological Engagement with Sociorhetorical Interpretation
    Michael Trainor..45

Enacting Sociorhetorical Interpretation in the Island Nation of Samoa in Oceania
    Vaitusi Nofoaiga..57

Fāiā Analysis of Romans 13:1–7: Integrating a Samoan Perspective with
Sociorhetorical Interpretation
    Fatilua Fatilua..71

Part 3: Explorations in Africa and Asia

Intersectional Texture: Reconsidering Gender Critical Frameworks and Sociorhetorical Interpretation
    Johnathan Jodamus..89

An Exploration of Economic Rhetoric in the New Testament in Light of New Institutional Economics
    Alex Hon Ho Ip...101

Bibliography... 111
Contributors 129
Ancient Sources Index 131
Modern Authors Index 135
Subject Index.. 139

Acknowledgments

Fig. 1, p. 45: Map of the Great Barrier Reef showing results of aerial surveys for 911 reefs, from "Only 7% of the Great Barrier Reef Has Avoided Coral Bleaching." https://www.coralcoe.org.au/media-releases/only-7-of-the-great-barrier-reef-has-avoided-coral-bleaching. Permission granted by Professor Terry Hughes, Australian Research Council Centre of Excellence for Coral Reef Studies, James Cook University, Townsville, Queensland.

Fig. 2, p. 46: IPPC observations and summary of land and ocean temperature, sea level, from Figure 1.1 from Observed Changes and Their Causes. IPCC, 2014: *Climate Change 2014: Synthesis Report. Contribution of Working Groups I, II and III to the Fifth Assessment Report of the Intergovernmental Panel on Climate Change*. Core Writing Team, edited by R. K. Pachauri and L. A. Meyer. IPCC, Geneva, Switzerland, 151 pp. Permission granted by the Intergovernmental Panel on Climate Change Secretariat.

Fig. 3, p. 49: Robbins's Sociorhetorical Exploration of a Biblical Text, from Vernon K. Robbins, *The Tapestry of Early Christian Discourse: Rhetoric, Society and Ideology* (London: Routledge, 1996), 21. Permission granted by Routledge.

Fig. 4, p. 49: Wainwright's adjustment to Robbins's Sociorhetorical Approach, from Elaine M. Wainwright, *Habitat, Human, and Holy: An Eco-rhetorical Reading of the Gospel of Matthew*, EBC 6 (Sheffield: Sheffield Phoenix, 2016), 25. Permission granted by Sheffield Phoenix Press.

Fig. 1, p. 62: Robbins's Sociorhetorical Model of Textual Interpretation, from Vernon K. Robbins, *The Tapestry of Early Christian Discourse: Rhetoric, Society and Ideology* (London: Routledge, 1996), 21. Permission granted by Routledge.

Abbreviations

BDAG	Danker, Frederick W., Walter Bauer, William F. Arndt, and F. Wilbur Gingrich. *A Greek-English Lexicon of the New Testament and Other Early Christian Literature*. 3rd ed. Chicago: University of Chicago Press, 2000.
BibInt	Biblical Interpretation Series
BR	*Biblical Research*
BZNW	Beihefte zur Zeitschrift für die neutestamentliche Wissenschaft
DTT	*Dansk teologisk tidsskrift*
ESEC	Emory Studies in Early Christianity
GPBS	Global Perspectives on Biblical Scholarship
HvTSt	*Hervormde teologiese studies*
Int	*Interpretation*
IPCC	Intergovernmental Panel on Climate Change
IVBS	International Voices in Biblical Studies
JBL	*Journal of Biblical Literature*
JECH	*Journal of Early Christian History*
JSNT	*Journal for the Study of the New Testament*
JSNTSup	Journal for the Study of the New Testament Supplement Series
Neot	*Neotestamentica*
NovT	*Novum Testamentum*
NovTSup	Supplements to Novum Testamentum
NRSV	New Revised Standard Version
NTS	*New Testament Studies*
RRA	Rhetoric of Religious Antiquity
SAC	Studies in Antiquity and Christianity
SBL	Society of Biblical Literature

SBLSP	Society of Biblical Literature Seminar Papers
SNTSMS	Society for New Testament Studies Monograph Series
SRI	Sociorhetorical Interpretation
SymS	Symposium Series
WUNT	Wissenschaftliche Untersuchungen zum Neuen Testament
ZABR	*Zeitschrift für altorientalische und biblische Rechtgeschichte*

Introduction

Vernon K. Robbins and Roy R. Jeal

The idea for this volume emerged after a Society of Biblical Literature session in 2017 featuring responses to *Foundations for Sociorhetorical Exploration*,[1] which appeared in 2016 as a twentieth anniversary celebration of the publication of *The Tapestry of Early Christian Discourse* and *Exploring the Texture of Texts* in 1996.[2] During the session, there were presentations by Duane F. Watson, Malone University; Shively T. J. Smith, Wesley Theological Seminary (now Boston University School of Theology); Raj Nadella, Columbia Theological Seminary; Alex Hon Ho Ip, Chinese University of Hong Kong; and Michael Trainor, Australian Catholic University. The report of Jione Havea, editor of the SBL Press International Voices in Biblical Studies series, at the SBL Press Book Series Editors meeting on the following morning prompted Vernon Robbins to consult about the possibility of expanding on the presentations of the day before to create a volume of essays on the international emergence of sociorhetorical interpretation (SRI).[3] The result is this volume, which contains three parts.

Part 1 focuses on the development and emergence of sociorhetorical interpretation. Duane Watson, who learned rhetorical interpretation of the New Testament from George A. Kennedy,[4] is the author of the initial essay, "Retro-

---

[1] SBL Rhetoric of Religious Antiquity Seminar, Retrospect and Prospects for Sociorhetorical Interpretation, S19-146, Boston, November 19, 2017. Vernon K. Robbins, Robert H. von Thaden, Jr., and Bart B. Bruehler, eds., *Foundations for Sociorhetorical Exploration: A Rhetoric of Religious Antiquity Reader*, RRA 4 (Atlanta: SBL Press, 2016).
[2] Vernon K. Robbins, *The Tapestry of Early Christian Discourse: Rhetoric, Society and Ideology* (New York: Routledge, 1996); Robbins, *Exploring the Texture of Texts: A Guide to the Socio-rhetorical Interpretation* (Harrisburg: Trinity Press International, 1996).
[3] SBL Press Book Series Editors, S20-102, Boston, November 20, 2017.
[4] George A. Kennedy, *New Testament Interpretation through Rhetorical Criticism* (Chapel Hill, NC: University of North Carolina Press, 1984).

spect and Prospect for Sociorhetorical Interpretation." Watson was instrumental in prompting Robbins and Samuel Byrskog, University of Göteborg, Sweden, to organize a five-year seminar in the Studiorum Novi Testamenti Societas (1999–2003), which created an international presence for sociorhetorical interpretation in several nations outside the United States.[5] In his essay, Watson describes the vibrant emergence of multiple approaches in biblical studies that were enriching the field of New Testament interpretation and were incorporated into sociorhetorical interpretation by Robbins and colleagues with whom he met regularly.

After Watson's essay, Robbins presents an account of the emergence of sociorhetorical interpretation outside the United States. Robbins has been in some of these locations, but many people who came into contact with the developing approach began to teach, adapt, and contribute to SRI in multiple international locations that reached far beyond Robbins's presence. Beginning in the 1990s with publications in Denmark, Canada, New Zealand, and the Czech Republic, SRI spread throughout South Africa with lectures and workshops by Robbins in nine universities during the summer of 1996. Then the five-year seminar on sociorhetorical interpretation in the Studiorum Novi Testamenti Societas mentioned above brought it to Israel, Great Britain, and Germany during 1999–2003. In the midst of this activity, the seven Pepperdine Conferences organized by Thomas H. Olbricht (1992–2002) brought significant interaction among sociorhetorical interpretation and neoclassical and feminist rhetorical interpretation in many international locations.[6]

Sociorhetorical interpretation gained further traction in Canada during the first decade of the twenty-first century through Rhetoric of Religious Antiquity meetings during a number of summers at Saint Paul University in Ottawa, where L. Gregory Bloomquist's students were writing PhD dissertations using sociorhetorical interpretation. During this time Roy R. Jeal at Booth University College, Winnipeg, became an active participant and author producing sociorhetorical publications. Also during this decade dissertations and books using sociorhetorical interpretation appeared in Hong Kong, Norway, Great Britain, and India, and during the second decade further works have appeared in Indonesia and Finland.

Robbins's essay ends with an account of the remarkable production of BD, MTh, and PhD theses in Samoa and Fiji by students using sociorhetorical interpretation. SRI was introduced in Oceania by Vaitusi Nofoaiga in 2007 following his studies with Professor Elaine Wainwright at the University of Auckland, New Zealand.

After Robbins's essay, Shively T. J. Smith brings part 1 to a close with an

---

[5] Pretoria, South Africa (1999); Tel Aviv, Israel (2000); Montreal, Canada (2001); Durham, UK (2002); Bonn, Germany (2003).
[6] Heidelberg, Germany (1992); Pretoria, South Africa (1994); London (1995); Malibu, California (1996); Florence, Italy (1998); Lund, Sweden (2000); Heidelberg (2002).

essay on strengths and gaps in the presentation of sociorhetorical interpretation in *Foundations for Sociorhetorical Exploration*. From her perspective, strengths are especially present in the approach to textures and the "ever-flowing streams of literary and historical, social and ideological, symbolic and semantic explorations of evolving Mediterranean religious discourses." What she perceives as a gap in the presentation in the volume is "its limited definition and use of what it considers anthropological and sociological resources for understanding the rhetorical nature of specific religious texts and its reverberating influences throughout history." In this context, she refers to Miranda Pillay's PhD dissertation that presents a sociorhetorical reading of the parable of the Good Samaritan in Luke 10:25–37 in relation to stigma in the context of HIV/AIDS in South Africa.[7] Smith considers this to be an example of the potential of sociorhetorical interpretation beyond its particular focus on Christianity during the first centuries of its emergence in Mediterranean society, culture, ideology, and religion. She proposes that SRI has a unique opportunity to broaden its uses of sociological and anthropological resources to make important contributions "in a global world at odds with itself because of ethnic discords, ever-growing suspicions of strangers and xenophobia, as well as unstable ecological systems, uneven distributions of global wealth, limited healthcare access, and ongoing failures to provide the basic needs necessary to ensure all humanity can live in dignity and flourish."

Part 2 focuses on particular applications of sociorhetorical interpretation in Australia and Oceania. The first essay in this section, written by Michael Trainor, describes how Elaine Wainwright reconfigured social-cultural texture in SRI into *ecological texture* to address the current threat of climate change on our world. Trainor focuses specifically on the Great Barrier Reef as a microcosm of this threat. He proposes that sociorhetorical interpretation should participate robustly in the ecotheological shift occurring in important circles in biblical studies by reclaiming interpretations like Saint Bede's (ca. 672–735 CE) who asserts that "every creature senses the Creator" in contrast to the majority of humans in the twenty-first century who have become "insensible" to the Creator. Trainor develops his essay with an account of "The Earth-Bible Project" and explains how Wainwright reworks Robbins's sociorhetorical model to create an "ecological climate" for interpretation of texts. Then he explains how Jon L. Berquist's essay on critical spatiality in the *Foundations for Sociorhetorical Exploration* volume can be used as a springboard for spatiality as "an eco-systemic reality" and Claudia Camp's essay on the temple can be used to focus on the temple as "an ecological firstspace." He ends his essay by using Bart Bruehler's essay in the volume on "social-spatial analysis of Luke" to introduce a summary

---

[7] Miranda Pillay, "Re-visioning Stigma: A Socio-rhetorical Reading of Luke 10:25–37 in the Context of HIV/AIDS in South Africa" (PhD diss., University of Western Cape, South Africa, 2008).

of his own approach to the story of Zacchaeus and the sycamore tree, which resonates with his ecological publications on the Gospel of Luke.[8]

After Trainor's essay, Vaitusi Nofoaiga describes how he is enacting sociorhetorical interpretation in Oceania. Explaining how he uses SRI within a hermeneutic from his island nation of Samoa, he introduces readers to his approach to discipleship in the gospels with special focus on his interpretation of Matthew. Using Samoan words related to Samoan social and cultural values, beliefs, practices, and institutions, he refers to the hermeneutic of *tautuaileva* (serve in-between spaces) and *fiaola* (opportunity seeker) as two means by which he has recently interpreted discipleship in the Gospel of Matthew.[9] Then he describes the special ways he uses "the interdisciplinary, multifaceted, and self-conscious practices of interpretation and reflection." This includes exploring the four primary textures of sociorhetorical analysis and interpretation, *topoi* with their special orientation to *place* in relation to the special rhetoric of place in Samoan oral traditions, rhetography with its special visual radical rhetoric, and the cognitive turn to conceptual blending in SRI.

Part 2 ends with an essay by Fatilua Fatilua on a Samoan SRI interpretation of Rom 13:1–7 in the context of the vote of the Samoan legislature in 2017 to declare American Samoa a Christian nation under a Triune God. Using the Samoan word *fāiā* (bridge), which conveys a sense of connection or relation, he describes the communal responsibility for Samoans to embody interconnectedness in all they do. Adding the concept of *upu* (word, text, speech language), he emphasizes the usefulness of language and the function of *fatua'iupu* (keepers of myths) for transmitting traditional knowledge in chants, songs, and other traditional compositions among the people. A major responsibility of the keepers of myths is to show tolerance to change while insisting on connecting it to "life justification proof, the life sources or *lagisoifua*" and the institution of *fatua'iupu*, which is built up from the word *fatu* (heart, core) and means to compose or construct in the sense of laying up in the memory or composing and committing to memory. In a context of the recognition that knowledge and language traverse both space and time, the *fāiā* approach "connotes exploring relations and connections in words, word constructions, and meaning." Once Fatilua has introduced this overall hermeneutical approach for his interpretation, he describes how his work for almost a decade in the gridlock and stalemate in the US Congress and his occupation of ongoing thirdspace in a hybrid world currently inspires him to employ this approach in recent events in his homeland. After analyzing and interpreting inner, progressive, argumentative, and social

---

[8] Michael Trainor, *Voices from the Edge: Luke's Gospel in Our World* (North Blackburn, Australia: Collins Dove, 1991); Trainor, *About Earth's Child: An Ecological Listening to the Gospel of Luke*, Earth Bible Commentary 2 (Sheffield: Sheffield Phoenix, 2012).

[9] Vaitusi Nofoaiga, *A Samoan Reading of Discipleship in Matthew*, IVBS 8 (Atlanta: SBL Press, 2017).

and cultural textures in Rom 13:1–7, he uses *feagaiga*, which has a range of meanings including "to be opposite to each other," "to correspond," or "to dwell together cordially," to explore challenges, opportunities, and responsibilities he perceives to be present in a context where the church is becoming marginalized by being placed outside of the political realm and disempowered within society.

Johnathan Jodamus's essay on gender critical frameworks opens part 3, which features uses of SRI in Africa and Asia. With a focus on reconfiguring SRI in the South African context, Jodamus describes challenges of being a black scholar among the majority of white scholarly interpreters of the New Testament in South Africa. Out of his experience of using SRI to interpret gender frameworks in his Master's thesis and PhD dissertation, and then teaching graduate courses during recent years, Jodamus proposes intersectional texture as an addition to sociorhetorical interpretation. *Intersectional texture*, a term coined during the 1990s by analogy to an intersection of streets where vehicles may be traveling in many directions, strives to analyze multiple forms of oppression and marginalization in a matrix of structural, hegemonic, and interpersonal domains of power that involve race, gender, class, ethnicity, and nationality. This approach, he proposes, moves beyond the positionality of ideological texture in SRI into a "thinking technology" that focuses on the multiplicity and interdependence of social factors that participate in creating and sustaining power relations that function as discourses in the making of normativities, identities, and social relations. Identifying types of bodies and *bodiliness* that are constructed and cultivated in contemporary society, Jodamus considers this analytical tool an advance to Robbins's own focus on relationalism in his emphasis that SRI is an interpretive analytics rather than a method with limited research objectives.

The final essay in the volume is written from the perspective of living in Hong Kong for many years, which the author of the essay Alex Hon Ho Ip calls the world's most capitalist economy. Using New Institutional Economics (NIE), developed in recent decades by Douglass North, Ip presents a critique of past uses of economic theory by Karl Polanyi, Michael Rostovtzeff, and Moses Finley to interpret economic factors at play in the ancient Mediterranean world. Rather than focusing on markets, NIE concentrates on multiple institutions that constrain rules and regulations on the basis of moral and ethical norms. This creates a framework for Ip to introduce *economic texture* within sociorhetorical strategies of analysis to interpret nuances of the Apostle Paul's argumentation with Philemon about his slave Onesimus. His approach includes household relationships in the context of Roman values and beliefs to interpret the value of Onesimus to Philemon and to exhibit the special force of Paul's rhetoric in the Mediterranean world of the first century CE. Most of all, Ip's goal is to open greater space to read the rhetoric of New Testament texts in relation to different layers of economics. In particular, this helps interpreters understand how metaphorical and figurative language are embedded in the economic realities of life in the ancient Mediterranean world and are internal to values and beliefs promoted by the authors of New Testament writings and in our world today.

The international voices heard in this volume tell us that many wonderful and unexpected things have been generated in the work of scholars literally from around the world through their sociorhetorical interpretations. We could scarcely have guessed at the innovative ideas and interpretations that have risen up through thinking about the rhetoric of textures, topoi, cultural geography and critical spatiality, conceptual blending, modes of discourse, and visual imagery that emerges when people in diverse places and cultures use SRI analytics in their readings of biblical texts. It reminds us of the importance of always being conscious that many things are unforeseen. The products of SRI amaze because they take us beyond what we know to new surprises of meaning. They press on us to expect to learn more than what was previously imagined. The voices heard here point us toward new and valuable varieties of interpretation and biblical commentary that use interpretive analytics rather than method derived from classical or modern rhetoric. They envision the reshaping and renuancing of the practice of interpretation that takes into account the multiple textures of texts.

The aim of sociorhetorical analytics is not to come to direct and clear answers to historical, sociohistorical, structural, ethical, or theological questions, most of which are not fully or clearly answerable. The goal is to identify, analyze, and interpret what the texts *do* and how they go about *doing* it. The concern, in other words, is about understanding the rhetorical force of New Testament and early Christian documents as they emerged, about how they are powerful in moving humans toward belief and wise behavior. So the SRI analytics are heuristic rather than being designed in the first place to define historical and theological truth, provide apologetic, or offer pastoral counsel. Questions of historical truth are crucial and we do not disparage what has been done. But they are not the only questions. The aim of SRI is not the determination of final knowledge (see 1 Cor 8:1b–3). The interpretive analytics are not a kind of scientific method where hypotheses anticipate the domains of conclusions in repeatable experimentation. Their goal, rather, is to find information and discover how it works. Discovery leads to more seeking, not to final definitions or, as Sirach tells us, "When human beings have finished, they are just beginning, and when they stop, they are still perplexed" (Sir 18:7). Discovering how texts work along with the vast range of their implications goes a long way toward understanding their more elusive theological and religious truth and power. They not only say things, they move people to think and act. They cause things to happen. The essays in this volume lead readers in this direction.

New textures of discourse are inevitable when new cultural and religious phenomena appear and when new ways of seeing ideas emerge. People develop new terminology and new language to talk about the beliefs and ways of life they encounter. The texts of the New Testament themselves offer reconfigured and even new textures and topoi as ways of talking about the new Christian faith. They employ wisdom, prophetic, precreational, priestly, apocalyptic, miracle and other religious textures. The history of interpretation demonstrates that this sort of thing has happened many times. The new textures reveal new knowledge certainly to interpreters and also to those taught by them, or, better, they reveal things previously *unknown* or *unrecognized*. These essays do the same thing, particularly in the ways the new analytical textures move us away from what Trainor correctly names as "anthropocentric" to consideration of places, persons, and ideas outside of ourselves. So we recognize ecological texture, intersectional texture, economic texture, and more localized Samoan linguistic and cultural textures of family, community, and politics, all of which have implications for anthropological and sociological world issues. This means that New Testament texts have things to say and meanings to impart about what goes on in our world, even if they sometimes speak in subtle ways. All this points out that the New Testament is not a book of propositions and narrow moralistic directives, but is a rhetoric of life in God's creation. The intellectual work of authors of the New Testament had a higher purpose than providing a rule book for believers. What they wanted to do was win over the hearts and minds of people, to change their lives. The New Testament aims to stir the imagination. To see it as less than this is reductionistic and anthropocentric.

So this volume offers some unexpected ideas revealed by SRI, some surprises of analysis. Who would have predicted the kinds of textures that have emerged? Yet, after all, perhaps we should not be so surprised, because careful readers of the ancient books know to expect more from the texts than they bring to them. The essays in this book point to the richness and ever-expanding possibilities for sociorhetorical commentary and the learning that enriches all of us.

Part 1
Development and Emergence of International Sociorhetorical Interpretation

Retrospect and Prospect of Sociorhetorical Interpretation

Duane F. Watson

Sociorhetorical interpretation (SRI) is primarily the product of one very creative scholar, Vernon K. Robbins, who long ago recognized the limitations of the historical-critical method and set out to broaden the horizons of biblical interpretation—and SRI does just that in quite amazing ways.[1] SRI also transcends the limitations of rhetorical analysis of the New Testament that is too dependent on classical rhetoric and its categories of judicial, deliberative, and epideictic that are drawn, respectively, from the courtroom, political assembly, and civic ceremonial settings in the city-state. These settings are largely foreign to the early church and its literature where the settings were the body, household, temple, and empire among others.

SRI is not a method predicated on a set of assumptions accompanied by a prescribed system of steps to follow for analyzing a text. Rather, SRI is a heuristic or interpretive analytic that enables interpreters to select from a variety of interpretive strategies and methods. These strategies and methods do not dominate the analysis of a text but are constantly reevaluated for their usefulness as the analysis progresses. SRI incorporates disciplines that tend to work in isolation from biblical studies or in isolated circles within biblical studies, and enables these disciplines to dialogue with one another. These disciplines include semiotics, sociolinguistics, literary studies, rhetoric, ethnography, social sciences, cognitive science, and ideological studies. With these disciplines, SRI pursues the rhetorical, social, cultural, ideological, and religious aspects of a text.

Robbins's essay on the sea voyages in Acts published in 1975 began to lay the groundwork for SRI.[2] He moved the discussion of the sea voyages in Acts

---

[1] For a detailed history of the development of SRI, see Vernon K. Robbins, "Sociorhetorical Interpretation," in *The Blackwell Companion to The New Testament*, ed. David E. Aune (Chichester, UK: Wiley-Blackwell, 2010), 192–219.

[2] Vernon K. Robbins, "The We-Passages in Acts and Ancient Sea Voyages," *BR* 20 (1975): 5–18. Also see Robbins, "By Land and By Sea: a Study in Acts 13–28," *SBLSP*

beyond the intertexture with Homer's *Odyssey* and Virgil's *Aeneid* to the broader social and cultural intertexture of sea voyage narratives in the Mediterranean world.[3] Robbins's book, *Jesus the Teacher: A Socio-rhetorical Interpretation of Mark*, published in 1984, laid more groundwork for incorporating the disciplines of rhetoric, sociology, and anthropology into biblical studies to dialogue with literary and historical exegesis.[4] He discovered a "teaching-learning" cycle in the Gospel of Mark that is found in the literature of the broader Mediterranean world. This literature includes works of Philo and Josephus, rabbinic literature, Plato's *Dialogues*, Xenophon's *Memorabilia*, Philostratus's *Life of Apollonius*, and Dio Chrysostom's *Discourses*. Robbins cast his net more widely into Mediterranean literature than was customary at the time.

In the 1980s and early 1990s Robbins's casting of the net beyond the Jewish Scriptures into the literature of the Mediterranean world incorporated the *progymnasmata* to analyze the creation of argumentation in the New Testament. This was particularly true of the exercise for the elaboration of the *chreia* within the *progymnasmata* which included recitation, inflection, commentary, objection, antithesis, expansion, condensation, and refutation or confirmation of the *chreia*. It was recognized that the gospel writers used this elaboration pattern to present the words and deeds of Jesus. Robbins was a central figure in this incorporation of the *progymnasmata* into New Testament studies, producing among other works, *Patterns of Persuasion in the Gospels* with Burton Mack.[5]

In this same period, New Testament scholarship was moving in many new and exciting directions. The New Testament was being analyzed from the perspective of rhetoric (Hans Dieter Betz; George Kennedy),[6] sociology (Wayne Meeks; Abraham Malherbe),[7] anthropology (Bryan Wilson),[8] and ideology

---

15 (1976): 381–96; and Robbins, "By Land and By Sea: The We-Passages and Ancient Sea Voyages," in *Perspectives on Luke-Acts*, ed. Charles H. Talbert (Macon, GA: Mercer University Press; Edinburgh: T&T Clark, 1978), 215–42.

[3] See Vernon K. Robbins, *Sea Voyages and Beyond: Emerging Strategies in Sociorhetorical Interpretation,* ESEC 14 (Atlanta: SBL Press, 2018), 47–113; Robbins, "Voyaging on the Sea of Life: Reflections on the We-Passages in Acts," *BR* 65 (2020): 58–76.

[4] Vernon K. Robbins, *Jesus the Teacher: A Socio-rhetorical Interpretation of Mark* (Philadelphia: Fortress, 1984).

[5] Burton Mack and Vernon K. Robbins, *Patterns of Persuasion in the Gospels* (Sonoma, CA: Polebridge Press, 1989).

[6] Hans Dieter Betz, *Galatians: A Commentary on Paul's Letter to the Churches in Galatia*, Hermeneia (Philadelphia; Fortress, 1979); George A. Kennedy, *New Testament Interpretation through Rhetorical Criticism* (Chapel Hill, NC: University of North Carolina Press, 1984).

[7] Wayne Meeks, *The First Urban Christians: The Social World of the Apostle Paul* (New Haven: Yale University Press, 1983); Abraham J. Malherbe, *Social Aspects of Early Christianity*, 2nd ed. (Philadelphia: Fortress, 1983).

(Wilhelm Wuellner; Elisabeth Schüssler Fiorenza).[9] Robbins utilized insights from these and other scholars to create his textures of texts. These textures premiered in 1992 in the introduction of the paperback edition of *Jesus the Teacher*.[10] They are the inner texture, intertexture, social and cultural texture, and ideological texture. These textures enable the interpreter to explore the network of meaning in a text.

Foundational for the discussion of the textures of texts is Robbins's essay, "Socio-rhetorical Criticism: Mary, Elizabeth, and the Magnificat as a Test Case" published in 1994.[11] In this essay, Robbins analyzed Luke 1:26–56 using his four textures, demonstrating how they work together. For example, he expanded the intertextual search from the Old Testament accounts of barren women to Greco-Roman accounts of the sexually violated and reconceived the Magnificat as reformist rather than revolutionist in its approach.

The textures were elaborated more fully in Robbins's 1996 works, *The Tapestry of Early Christian Discourse* and *Exploring the Texture of Texts*.[12] The latter added sacred texture. Inner texture is adapted from modern literary analysis and involves the structure of a text, including word patterns, literary devices, argumentation, and literary progressions. Intertexture, to quote Robbins, "is a text's representation of, reference to, and use of phenomena in the 'world' outside the text being interpreted. In other words, the intertexture of a text is the interaction of the language in the text with 'outside' material and physical 'objects,' historical events, texts, customs, values, roles, institutions, and systems."[13] Social and cultural texture is the social and cultural location of the systems, institutions, and values the text presupposes and evokes and how the text relates to the dominant culture. Ideological texture involves the assumptions

---

[8] Bryan R. Wilson, *Magic and the Millennium: A Sociological Study of Religious Movements of Protest among Tribal and Third-World Peoples* (New York: Harper & Row, 1973).

[9] Wilhelm Wuellner, "Hermeneutics and Rhetorics: From 'Truth and Method' to 'Truth and Power,'" *Scriptura* 3 (1989): 1–54; Elisabeth Schüssler Fiorenza, "The Ethics of Interpretation: De-Centering Biblical Scholarship," *JBL* 107 (1988): 3–17.

[10] Vernon K. Robbins, introduction to *Jesus the Teacher: A Socio-rhetorical Interpretation of Mark* (Minneapolis: Fortress, 1992), xix–xliv.

[11] Vernon K. Robbins, "Socio-rhetorical Criticism: Mary, Elizabeth, and the Magnificat as a Test Case," in *Foundations for Sociorhetorical Exploration: A Rhetoric of Religious Antiquity Reader*, ed. Vernon K. Robbins, Robert H. von Thaden Jr., and Bart B. Bruehler, RRA 4 (Atlanta: SBL Press, 2016), 29–74.

[12] Vernon K. Robbins, *The Tapestry of Early Christian Discourse: Rhetoric, Society and Ideology* (New York: Routledge, 1996). Vernon K. Robbins, *Exploring the Texture of Texts: A Guide to Socio-rhetorical Interpretation* (Harrisburg, PA: Trinity Press International, 1996).

[13] Robbins, *Exploring the Texture of Texts*, 40.

and values implicit or expressed in a text that sustain power structures. Sacred texture concerns how a text views religious belief and practice.

The decade after 1996 was a time of much dialogue and exploration. Analyzing a text with the textures revealed that the overall texture of Christian discourse varied considerably. Robbins identified and described six types of early Christian discourse that he labeled *rhetorolects*, an elision of *rhetorical dialects*. A rhetorolect is "a form of language variety or discourse identifiable on the basis of a distinctive configuration of themes, topics, reasonings and argumentations."[14] The six rhetorolects of early Christian discourse subsequently identified are wisdom, prophetic, apocalyptic, precreation, miracle, and priestly. For example, wisdom rhetorolect is discourse that blends human experience with belief about God and the cosmos from the perspective of the household where parents teach their children how to live fruitfully and faithfully. In this rhetorolect God becomes the teacher of all Christians seen as children within God's household. Early Christian authors blended these rhetorolects in different ways to create Christian discourse.

During the 1990s there was also a focus in scholarship on the reasoning of early Christian discourse, particularly the enthymeme. This discussion moved beyond seeing an enthymeme as a stated premise, unstated or assumed premise, and a conclusion to a more comprehensive understanding of how enthymemes use and reconfigure social, cultural, ideological, and theological topics and values, using some to reconfigure others.[15] The result was analyzing enthymemes as rule, case, and result, and participation in the broader discussion of the nature of deductive, inductive, and abductive reasoning in early Christian argumentation.

By 2000 it became apparent that each of the six rhetorolects elaborated *topoi* and created enthymematic argumentation differently. Robbins outlined the enthymematic argumentative elaboration in the six rhetorolects.[16] He began to identify two types of elaboration within the rhetorolects: narrative-descriptive and argumentative-enthymematic. Cognitive science gave Robbins the tools to refine this initial identification further, particularly with the work of Gilles Fauconnier and Mark Turner, *The Way We Think: Conceptual Blending and the Mind's Hidden Complexities*.[17] The narrative-descriptive element of a rhetorolect

---

[14] Vernon K. Robbins, "The Dialectical Nature of Early Christian Discourse," *Scriptura* 59 (1996): 356.

[15] Vernon K. Robbins, "The Present and Future of Rhetorical Analysis," in *The Rhetorical Analysis of Scripture: Essays from the 1995 London Conference*, ed. Stanley E. Porter and Thomas H. Olbricht, JSNTSup 146 (Sheffield: Sheffield Academic, 1997), 33–40.

[16] Vernon K. Robbins, "Argumentative Textures in Socio-rhetorical Interpretation," in *Rhetorical Argumentation in Biblical Texts*, ed. Anders Eriksson, Thomas H. Olbricht, and Walter Übelacker, ESEC 8 (Harrisburg, PA: Trinity Press International, 2002), 27–65.

[17] Gilles Fauconnier and Mark Turner, *The Way We Think: Conceptual Blending and the Mind's Hidden Complexities* (New York: Basic Books, 2002).

became known as rhetography, and the argumentative-enthymematic element of a rhetorolect became known as rhetology.[18] These worked together and differently within each rhetorolect to further the rhetorical purposes of the author.

Rhetography focuses on how a text creates images in the mind of the reader or hearer, images that have their own persuasive power. The text produces a series of images in succession that create a storyline. Each rhetorolect has a basic shared storyline or rhetography. For example, apocalyptic rhetorolect pictures an imperial army sent out by a king to destroy rebellious elements of the empire in order to reestablish peace and salvation. Rhetology is the argumentation of a text with enthymemes or elaboration of a thesis using rationale, opposite, analogy, example, citation of an author, and/or conclusion as found in the *progymnasmata*. Furthermore, each of the rhetorolects has a distinctive way of blending rhetography and rhetology.

It became apparent that the rhetology and rhetography within the rhetorolects was emerging from picturing and reasoning drawn from various social, cultural, and ideological places to create enthymematic argumentation. These places included intersubjective bodies, households, villages, synagogues, cities, temples, kingdoms, empires, the world, and the cosmos. The pictures and reasoning in argumentation were coming from lives lived in specific places in the Mediterranean world, not the places of the city-state—courtroom, political assembly, and civil ceremony—as was formal rhetoric. In other words, the topography of early Christian discourse was different from classical rhetoric. The temple was the place of priestly rhetorolect, the body of miracle rhetorolect, the imperial household of apocalyptic rhetorolect, the domestic household of wisdom rhetorolect, a kingdom of prophetic rhetorolect, and the emperor of precreation rhetorolect.

To focus these observations, Robbins turned to cultural geography, particularly critical spatiality theory, as found, among others, in Robert Sack, T. F. Carney, Henri Lefebvre, and Edward W. Soja.[19] Cultural geography studies the interaction between culture and its created places and interpreted or imagined spaces. People experience places which they interpret as social, cultural, ideological, and religious spaces. Each rhetorolect has a different blend of cultural

---

[18] Vernon K. Robbins, "Rhetography: A New Way of Seeing the Familiar Text," in *Words Well Spoken: George Kennedy's Rhetoric of the New Testament*, ed. C. Clifton Black and Duane F. Watson, Studies in Rhetoric and Religion 8 (Waco, TX: Baylor University Press, 2008), 91–106; repr. Robbins, von Thaden, and Bruehler, *Foundations for Sociorhetorical Exploration*, 367–92.

[19] Robert Sack, *Human Territoriality: In Theory and History* (Cambridge: Cambridge University Press, 1986). T. F. Carney, *The Shape of the Past: Models and Antiquity* (Lawrence, KS: Coronado Press, 1975); Henri Lefebvre, *The Production of Space* (Oxford: Blackwell, 1991); Edward W. Soja, *Thirdspace: Journeys to Los Angeles and Other Real-and-Imagined Places* (Oxford: Blackwell, 1996).

geography, of social places with cultural, ideological, and religious spaces. Each rhetorolect has a different configuration of topics to negotiate places to create social, cultural, ideological, and religious spaces.

To cultural geography and critical spatiality theory Robbins added conceptual blending theory from cognitive science, again leaning on Fauconnier and Turner's *The Way We Think*.[20] This union helped explain the relationship of social places to cultural, ideological, and religious spaces and their different blends within the six Christian rhetorolects. Not only that, but it helped explain how Early Christian discourse blends the rhetorolects themselves and their spaces to evoke new pictures, emotions, and reasonings that have rhetorical force. These rhetorolects and their associated rhetography and rhetology do not typically work in isolation, but blend together. Their topics, reasonings, and picturing blend to form what Robbins calls "emergent structures." These give rhetorical force to a text.

Recently, Robbins further refined the conceptualization of rhetorolects, viewing them as localized blends within the three categories of Mediterranean religious discourse: mythical, philosophical, and ritual as described by Varro (ca. 45 BCE). Christians produced localized versions of these three categories of Mediterranean religious discourse. Prophetic and apocalyptic rhetorolects are localizations of mantic discourse involving communication from the divine, with the prophetic rhetorolect emphasizing the oracular and the apocalyptic rhetorolect emphasizing the visual. Wisdom and precreation rhetorolects localize philosophical discourse, with the wisdom rhetorolect emphasizing moral philosophy and the precreation rhetorolect emphasizing speculative philosophy. Priestly and miracle rhetorolects localize ritual discourse, with the priestly rhetorolect emphasizing sacrifice and mystery, and the miracle rhetorolect emphasizing healing. For an example of this localization, early Christian wisdom rhetorolect localizes Mediterranean moral philosophical discourse. It blends the household and the world with God's cosmos. In this blend, God is the heavenly Father over God's children who are to use God's wisdom to bring righteousness and wisdom into the world.[21]

During the past decade, much deliberation has centered on how to create sustained commentary on biblical and other literature using SRI. This work was spurred on by the formation of the Rhetoric of Religious Antiquity Series of commentaries published by SBL Press. In brief, the most helpful form of presentation of SRI to emerge is the presentation of the rhetography and rhetorolects of

---

[20] See also Robbins's essay, "Conceptual Blending and Early Christian Imagination," in Robbins, von Thaden, and Bruehler, *Foundations for Sociorhetorical Exploration*, 329–64.

[21] For a brief synopsis of the blends of all six Christian rhetorolects, see Robbins, "Socio-Rhetorical Interpretation," 200–203.

a text first, then the discussion of the textures of the text, and finally the analysis of the rhetorical force of the text that the blending of textures and rhetorolects creates.

The first step is to describe the rhetography of a text. Begin with the sequence of the pictures that a discourse evokes as rhetorolects and their picturing are blended. For example, as Robbins has shown, in the opening of 2 Peter in 1:1–11, "Peter functions as prophet, priest, sage, agent of God's power, and apocalyptic seer. In turn, his hearers are members of God's kingdom on earth, recipients of priestly holiness, possessors of wisdom from God, benefactors of God's miraculous powers, and visionaries of God's eternal kingdom."[22] This initial step of picturing is followed by an analysis of the textures of the text to show how the rhetography and rhetology of the text work together. Here, in whatever order best suits the explication of the text, the interpreter explores inner texture, inter texture, social and cultural texture, and ideological texture of the text as discussed in Robbins's earlier works.[23] Finally, SRI discusses the rhetorical force of the text as emergent Christian discourse. It explores how the blending of the rhetography and rhetology of the rhetorolects reconfigures Mediterranean discourse to create new reality.

Along the path of its development, SRI has been utilized to analyze texts outside the field of biblical studies, such as the Babylonian Talmud and the Mishnah,[24] and that trend will continue. Also, as Vernon developed SRI, his infectious and gracious spirit gathered, nurtured, and enriched many younger scholars whom he brought into dialogue with him. Many of these younger scholars are members of the Rhetoric of Religious Antiquity Group who share a unique privilege of scholarly collaboration and friendship that we owe to Vernon and, in many cases, have continued to enjoy for nearly thirty years. Vernon's collaboration models SRI in inviting scholars from an amazing diversity of institutions and specialties to dialogue with him and discover new and more comprehensive things in biblical interpretation. SRI will continue to be refined and contribute even more to biblical studies in the future as the essays in this volume attest.

---

[22] Robbins, "Socio-rhetorical Interpretation," 205.
[23] Robbins, *Tapestry of Early Christian Discourse*, 44–236; Robbins, *Exploring the Texture of Texts*, 7–119.
[24] Jack N. Lightstone, *The Rhetoric of the Babylonian Talmud: Its Social Meaning and Context*, Studies in Christianity and Judaism/Études sur le christianisme et le judaïsme 6 (Waterloo: Wilfrid Laurier University Press for the Canadian Corporation for Studies in Religion/Corporation Canadienne des Sciences Religieuses, 1994); Lightstone, *Mishnah and the Social Formation of the Early Rabbinic Guild: A Socio-rhetorical Approach*, Studies in Christianity and Judaism/Études sur le christianisme et le judaïsme 6 (Waterloo: Wilfrid Laurier University Press for the Canadian Corporation for Studies in Religion/Corporation Canadienne des Sciences Religieuses, 2002).

From Otago, Africa, and India to Asia, Australia, and Oceania

Vernon K. Robbins

During the past decades various essays have been written on the emergence of sociorhetorical interpretation (SRI). The first account appeared as an introduction to the paperback edition of *Jesus the Teacher* (1992), which in its initial publication in 1984 launched sociorhetorical interpretation in New Testament studies.[1] In 1994, Vernon K. Robbins displayed sociorhetorical textural commentary based on four textures,[2] and David B. Gowler wrote a programmatic account of the development of sociorhetorical interpretation.[3] In 1998–1999, Duane F. Watson and H. J. Bernard Combrink published major essays on sociorhetorical interpretation and in 2002 on sociorhetorical commentary.[4] Two overviews appeared in 2004 and

---

[1] Vernon K. Robbins, introduction to *Jesus the Teacher: A Socio-rhetorical Interpretation of Mark* (Minneapolis: Fortress, 1992), xix–xliv.

[2] Vernon K. Robbins, "Socio-rhetorical Criticism: Mary, Elizabeth, and the Magnificat as a Test Case," in *The New Literary Criticism and the New Testament*, ed. Elizabeth Struthers Malbon and Edgar V. McKnight (Sheffield: Sheffield Academic, 1994), 164–209, repr. *Foundations for Sociorhetorical Exploration: A Rhetoric of Religious Antiquity Reader*, ed. Vernon K. Robbins, Robert H. von Thaden Jr., and Bart B. Bruehler, RRA 4 (Atlanta: SBL Press, 2016), 29–74.

[3] David B. Gowler, "The Development of Socio-rhetorical Criticism," in *New Boundaries in Old Territory: Form and Social Rhetoric in Mark*, ed. Vernon K. Robbins and David B. Gowler, ESEC 3 (New York: Lang, 1994), 1–36.

[4] Duane F. Watson, "Vernon Robbins' Socio-rhetorical Criticism: A Review," *JSNT* 70 (1998): 67–115; H. J. Bernard Combrink, "The Challenge of Making and Redrawing Boundaries: A Perspective on Socio-rhetorical Criticism," *Nederduitse Gereformeerde Teologiese Tydskrif* 40 (1999): 18–30; Combrink, "The Challenges and Opportunities of a Socio-rhetorical Commentary," *Scriptura* 79 (2002): 106–21; Watson, "Why We Need Socio-rhetorical Commentary and What It Might Look Like," in *Rhetorical Criticism and the Bible*, ed. Stanley E. Porter and Dennis L. Stamps, JSNTSup 195 (Sheffield: Sheffield Academic, 2002), 129–57.

2006,[5] and three more appeared in 2010 and another in 2013.[6] In 2014, Troy W. Martin's *Genealogies of New Testament Rhetorical Criticism*, which featured "five pioneers of rhetorical criticism," contained a programmatic essay on sociorhetorical interpretation by L. Gregory Bloomquist and a response by Robbins.[7] The present essay supplements the essays referred to above by focusing on the emergence of sociorhetorical interpretation beyond the borders of the United States. Starting in Canada and New Zealand, it moves to South Africa and then on to other countries, ending with special recent developments in Samoa and Fiji. I offer this information with gratitude and amazement at the ease with which it is now possible to communicate promptly with international colleagues at far distances from my Atlanta office in the United States.

It appears that the first publication by an international scholar specifically addressing sociorhetorical interpretation may be Jørgen Skafte Jensen's "Retorisk kritik: Om en ny vej I evangelieforskningen" in 1992, which he wrote after spending a research sabbatical from the University of Copenhagen at Emory University, where he attended my PhD seminar on Rhetorical Criticism in the New Testament.[8] Then 1993–94 were the first years in my records when international studies using SRI reached a completed stage in PhD dissertations. In 1993, Willi Braun completed his PhD dissertation at the University of Toronto on the banquet in the house of a leader of the Pharisees in Luke 14:1–24. His sociorhetorical approach gave special attention to the man with dropsy whom Jesus heals at the beginning of the account. In Mediterranean tradition, Braun argues, the man would have

---

[5] Vernon K. Robbins, "Beginnings and Developments in Socio-rhetorical Interpretation," 1 May 2004, http://tinyurl.com/SBL7103h; W. Randolph Tate, "Socio-rhetorical Criticism," in *Interpreting the Bible: A Handbook of Terms and Methods* (Peabody, MA: Hendrickson, 2006), 342–46.

[6] Vernon K. Robbins, "Socio-rhetorical Interpretation," in *The Blackwell Companion to the New Testament*, ed. David E. Aune, Blackwell Companions to Religion (Malden, MA: Wiley-Blackwell, 2010), 192–219; David B. Gowler, "The End of the Beginning: The Continuing Maturation of Socio-rhetorical Analysis," in *Sea Voyages and Beyond: Emerging Strategies in Socio-rhetorical Interpretation*, ed. Vernon K. Robbins, ESEC 14 (Atlanta: SBL Press, 2018), 1–45; Gowler, "Socio-rhetorical Interpretation: Textures of a Text and Its Reception," *JSNT* 33 (2010): 191–206; Robbins, "Socio-rhetorical Criticism," in *The Oxford Encyclopedia of Biblical Interpretation*, vol. 2 (New York: Oxford University Press, 2013), 311–18. Also see Vernon K. Robbins, "Sociorhetorical Interpretation and the New Testament," in *Oxford Handbook of New Testament Rhetoric*, ed. Mark D. Given (London: Oxford University Press, forthcoming).

[7] L. Gregory Bloomquist, "The Pesky Threads of Robbins's Rhetorical Tapestry: Vernon K. Robbins's Genealogy of Rhetorical Criticism," in *Genealogies of New Testament Rhetorical Criticism*, ed. Troy W. Martin (Minneapolis: Fortress, 2014), 201–24; Vernon K. Robbins, "From the Social Sciences to Rhetography," in Martin, *Genealogies*, 225–44.

[8] Jørgen Skafte Jensen, "Retorisk kritik: Om en ny vej I evangelieforskningen," *DTT* 55 (1992): 262–79; ET: "Rhetorical Criticism: On a New Way in Gospel Research."

been viewed symbolically as a greedy person, because people with dropsy were known for their insatiable thirst and hunger.[9] Then in 1994 Mary R. Huie-Jolly completed her PhD dissertation at the University of Otago, New Zealand on Jesus's discourse on his healing of the lame man in John 5:17–23. The dissertation was written in a New Zealand theological context influenced by a renaissance of indigenous Maori and Samoan cultural reflection. Within this emergent postcolonial context, her interest in the sociorhetorical contexts of absolute claims in John 5 originated in her feminist discomfort with strongly authoritarian controlling language in John's Gospel and its powerful rhetorical impact on hearers.[10] In subsequent postcolonial studies she explored the impact of British missionary culture, infused with divine imperial assumptions, upon Maori perceptions of "the crown."

Following these beginnings, two significant international publications appeared during 1995. Willi Braun published a revision of his doctoral dissertation as *Feasting and Social Rhetoric in Luke 14*.[11] In addition, István Czachesz, a citizen of Hungary, published an essay titled "Socio-rhetorical Exegesis of Acts 9:1–30" in the Czech Republic (Prague) after taking a seminar on "Socio-rhetorical Criticism of the New Testament" with me at Emory University as he was completing his MTh at Columbia Theological Seminary in Decatur, Georgia.[12] In later years, I published essays in Festschriften for Petr Pokorný at the Protestant Theological Faculty of Charles University in Prague and Zdeněk Sázava at the Hussite Theological Faculty of Charles University in Prague.[13]

---

[9] Willi Braun, "The Use of Mediterranean Banquet Traditions in Luke 14:1-24" (PhD diss., University of Toronto, 1993); also see Braun, "Social-rhetorical Interests: Context," in *Whose Historical Jesus?*, ed. William E. Arnal, Studies in Christianity and Judaism 7 (Waterloo ON: Wilfrid Laurier University Press, 1997), 93–95.

[10] Mary R. Huie-Jolly, "The Son Enthroned in Conflict: A Socio-rhetorical Analysis of John 5:17-23" (PhD diss., University of Otago, New Zealand, 1994); also Huie-Jolly, "Like Father, Like Son, Absolute Case, Mythic Authority: Constructing Ideology in John 5:17–23," in *Society of Biblical Literature 1997 Seminar Papers*, SBLSP 36 (Atlanta: Society of Biblical Literature, 1997), 567–95.

[11] Willi Braun, *Feasting and Social Rhetoric in Luke 14*, SNTSMS 85 (Cambridge: Cambridge University Press, 1995).

[12] István Czachesz, "Socio-rhetorical Exegesis of Acts 9:1–30," *Communio Viatorum* (Praha) 37 (1995): 5–32.

[13] Vernon K. Robbins, "Socio-rhetorical Hermeneutics and Commentary," in *EPI TO AYTO: Essays in honour of Petr Pokorny on His Sixty-Fifth Birthday*, ed. J. Mrazek, S. Brodsky, and R. Dvorakova (Praha-Trebenice: Mlyn Publishers, 1998), 284–97; Robbins, "The Socio-rhetorical Role of Old Testament Scripture in Luke 4–19," in *Z Noveho Zakona/From the New Testament: Sbornik k narozeninam Prof. ThDr. Zdenka Sazavy*, ed. Hana Tonzarova and Petr Melmuk (Praha: Vydala Cirkev ceskoslovenska husitska, 2001), 81–93.

Sociorhetorical research and publication started in South Africa after my first sojourn in universities there during 1996, sponsored and funded by the Centre for Science Development, Human Research Science Council, Johannesburg. In 1997 Martin J. Oosthuizen, from his location at Port Elizabeth, published an essay in a German *Zeitschrift* containing sociorhetorical interpretation of ordinances for remission of sins and manumission of slaves in Deut 15:1–18.[14] Then in 1999, Daphne Mathebula completed an MA thesis using sociorhetorical interpretation at the University of Johannesburg on Jonah's attitude toward socioreligious change.[15]

In 1999, Samuel Byrskog, University of Göteborg, Sweden, teamed with me to organize a five-year seminar on sociorhetorical interpretation at the international meetings of the Studiorum Novi Testamenti Societas. The first meeting of the seminar occurred at the University of Pretoria, South Africa, and subsequent meetings occurred in Tel Aviv (2000); Montreal (2001); Durham, UK (2002); and Bonn, Germany (2003). Prior to and during the years of this seminar, H. J. Bernard Combrink published the major essays on sociorhetorical criticism in South Africa mentioned above,[16] plus additional essays that displayed techniques of sociorhetorical commentary and sociorhetorical interpretive strategies for interpreting multiple institutional manifestations of Reformed theology in South Africa.[17] Combrink's publications, teaching, and oversight of the appointment of Robbins as a Visiting Professor at the University of Stellenbosch created an environment for a number of additional publications in South Africa.[18]

---

[14] Martin J. Oosthuizen, "Deuteronomy 15:1–18 in Socio-rhetorical Perspective," *ZABR* 3 (1997): 64–91.

[15] Daphne Mathebula, "Jonah's Attitude towards Socio-religious Change" (MA thesis, Johannesburg: University of Johannesburg, 1999).

[16] Combrink, "The Challenge of Making and Redrawing Boundaries: A Perspective on Socio-rhetorical Criticism"; Combrink, "The Challenges and Opportunities of a Socio-rhetorical Commentary."

[17] H. J. Bernard Combrink, "The Rhetoric of the Church in the Transition from the Old to the New South Africa: Socio-rhetorical Criticism and Ecclesiastical Rhetoric," *Neot* 32 (1998), 289–307; Combrink, "Shame on the Hypocritical Leaders in the Church: A Socio-rhetorical Interpretation of the Reproaches in Matthew 23," in *Fabrics of Discourse: Essays in Honor of Vernon K. Robbins*, ed. David B. Gowler, L. Gregory Bloomquist, and Duane F. Watson (Harrisburg, PA : Trinity Press International, 2003), 1–35; Combrink, "The Contribution of Socio-rhetorical Interpretation to the Reformed Interpretation of Scripture," in *Reformed Theology: Identity and Ecumenicity II: Biblical Interpretation in the Reformed Tradition*, ed. Wallace M. Alston Jr. and Michael Welker (Grand Rapids: Eerdmans, 2007), 91–106.

[18] Jung Sig Park, "The Shepherd Discourse in John 10: A Rhetorical Interpretation" (DTh diss., University of Stellenbosch, 1999); Chul Woo Lee, "A Socio-rhetorical Analysis of Romans 7: With Special Attention to the Law" (DTh diss., University of Stellenbosch, 2001); see also Lee, "Understanding the Law in Rom. 7:1–6: an Enthymemic Analysis,"

In addition, Gerhard van den Heever published a textbook guided by sociorhetorical interpretation at the University of South Africa, Pretoria, South Africa,[19] which became a resource for the production of a number of theses and publications by people who took a program of studies at this university.[20] Charles A. Wanamaker incorporated sociorhetorical interpretation into his own studies of the New Testament at the University of Cape Town, and his teaching and advising have borne fruit in theses at this university.[21]

In the midst of this, Miranda Pillay produced a PhD thesis on sociorhetorical interpretation of the parable of the Good Samaritan in Luke 10:25–37 in relation to HIV/AIDS in South Africa, cosupervised by Professor Elna Mouton at the University of Stellenbosch and Professor Ernst Conradie at the University of the Western Cape.[22] Other people also published sociorhetorical articles, and I agreed to write an essay on influences on me through interaction with African biblical scholars.[23]

Scriptura 88 (2005), 126–38; Marius Nel, "The Mysteries of the Kingdom of Heaven according to Matthew 13:10–17," *Neot* 43 (2009): 271–88.

[19] Gerhard van den Heever, *From Jesus Christ to Christianity: Early Christian Literature in Context* (Pretoria: UNISA Press, 2001); see also Heever, "Finding Data in Unexpected Places (Or: From Text Linguistics to Socio-rhetoric): A Socio-rhetorical Reading of John's Gospel," in *Society of Biblical Literature Seminar Papers*, SBLSP 37 (Atlanta: Society of Biblical Literature, 1998): 2:649–76; Heever, "'From the Pragmatics of Textures to a Christian Utopia': The Case of the Gospel of John," in *Rhetorical Criticism and the Bible*, ed. Stanley E. Porter and Dennis L. Stamps, JSNTSup 195 (Sheffield: Sheffield Academic, 2002), 297–334.

[20] R. P. Tupparainen, "The Role(s) of the Spirit-Paraclete in John 16:4b–15: A Sociorhetorical Investigation" (PhD diss., University of South Africa, Pretoria, 2007); David Jay Miller, "Characterisations of YHWH in the Song of the Vineyard: A Multitextual Interpretation of Isaiah 5:1–7" (PhD diss., University of South Africa, Pretoria, 2013); Benard N. Ombori, "A Socio-rhetorical Appraisal of Jesus as Sacrifice, with Specific Reference to *Hilasterion* in Romans 3:25–26" (MTh thesis, University of South Africa, Pretoria, 2013).

[21] Charles A. Wanamaker, "'By the Power of God': Rhetoric and Ideology in 2 Corinthians 10–13," in *Fabrics of Discourse: Essays in Honor of Vernon K. Robbins*, ed. David B. Gowler, L. Gregory Bloomquist, and Duane F. Watson (New York: Trinity Press International, 2003), 194–221; Johnathan Jodamus, "A Socio-rhetorical Exegesis of 1 Timothy 2.18–25" (MSocSci thesis, University of Cape Town, South Africa, 2005); Jodamus, "An Investigation into the Construction(s) and Representation(s) of Masculinity(ies) and Femininity(ies) in 1 Corinthians" (PhD diss., University of Capetown, South Africa, 2015); Kimseng Tan, *The Rhetoric of Abraham's Faith in Romans 4*, ESEC 20 (Atlanta: SBL Press, 2018).

[22] Miranda Pillay, "Re-visioning Stigma: A Socio-rhetorical Reading of Luke 10:25–37 in the Context of HIV/AIDS in South Africa" (PhD diss., University of Western Cape, South Africa, 2008).

[23] J. A. (Bobby) Loubser, "Invoking the Ancestors: Some Socio-rhetorical Aspects of the Genealogies in the Gospels of Mathew and Luke," *Neot* 39.1 (2005): 127–40; Annang

The international emergence of SRI was strongly facilitated by the robust advance of rhetorical interpretation of the New Testament in the seven Pepperdine Conferences organized by Thomas H. Olbricht from 1992 to 2002 (Heidelberg 1992; Pretoria 1994; London 1995; Malibu 1996; Florence 1998; Lund 2000; Heidelberg 2002).[24] L. Gregory Bloomquist, Saint Paul University, Ottawa, attended the London conference in 1995 and began working immediately with sociorhetorical analysis, hermeneutics, and interpretation.[25] His productive and distinctive work on sociorhetorical interpretation flourished 2000–2010.[26] Then he has

---

Asumang, "The Presence of the Shepherd: A Rhetographic Exegesis of Psalm 23," *Conspectus: The Journal of the South African Theological Seminar* 9 (2010): 1–23; Vernon K. Robbins, "Why Participate in African Biblical Interpretation?," in *Interpreting the New Testament in Africa*, ed. Mary N. Getui, Tinyiko S. Maluleke, and Justin Ukpong (Nairobi, Kenya: Acton Publishers, 2001), 275–91.

[24] Vernon K. Robbins, "From Heidelberg to Heidelberg: Rhetorical Interpretation of the Bible at the Seven 'Pepperdine' Conferences from 1992 to 2002," in *Rhetoric, Ethic and Moral Persuasion in Biblical Discourse*, ed. Thomas H. Olbricht and Anders Eriksson, ESEC 11 (New York: T&T Clark International, 2005), 335–77.

[25] L. Gregory Bloomquist, "Rhetorical Argumentation and the Culture of Apocalyptic: A Socio-rhetorical Analysis of Luke 21," in *The Rhetorical Interpretation of Scripture: Essays from the 1996 Malibu Conference*, ed. Stanley E. Porter and Dennis L. Stamps, JSNTSup 180 (Sheffield: Sheffield Academic, 1999), 173–209; Bloomquist, "Patristic Reception of a Lukan Healing Account: A Contribution to a Socio-rhetorical Response to Willi Braun's *Feasting and Social Rhetoric in Luke 14*, SNTSMS 85 (Cambridge: University Press, 1995)," in *Healing in Religion and Society, From Hippocrates to the Puritans*, ed. Stephen Muir and J. Kevin Coyle, Studies in Religion and Society 43 (Lewiston: Edwin Mellen Press, 1999), 105–34; Bloomquist, "Methodological Criteria for the Determination of Apocalyptic Rhetoric: A Suggestion for the Expanded Use of Socio-rhetorical Analysis," in *Vision and Persuasion: Rhetorical Dimensions of Early Jewish and Christian Apocalyptic Discourse*, ed. Greg Carey and L. Gregory Bloomquist (Saint Louis: Chalice, 1999), 181–203.

[26] L. Gregory Bloomquist, "A Possible Direction for Providing Programmatic Correlation of Textures in Socio-rhetorical Analysis," in *Rhetorical Criticism and the Bible*, ed. Stanley E. Porter and Dennis L. Stamps, JSNTSup 195 (Sheffield: Sheffield Academic, 2002), 61–96; Bloomquist, "The Role of the Audience in the Determination of Argumentation: The Gospel of Luke and the Acts of the Apostles," in *Rhetorical Argumentation in Biblical Texts: Essays from the Lund 2000 Conference*, ed. Anders Eriksson, Thomas H. Olbricht, and Walter Übelacker, ESEC 8 (Harrisburg: Trinity Press International, 2002), 157–73; Bloomquist, "The Intertexture of Lukan Apocalyptic Discourse," in *The Intertexture of Apocalyptic Discourse in the New Testament*, ed. Duane F. Watson, SymS 14 (Atlanta: Society of Biblical Literature, 2002), 45–68; Bloomquist, "Paul's Inclusive Language: The Ideological Texture of Romans 1," in *Fabrics of Discourse: Essays in Honor of Vernon K. Robbins*, ed. David B. Gowler, L. Gregory Bloomquist, and Duane F. Watson (New York: Trinity Press International, 2003), 165–93; repr., in Robbins, von Thaden, and Brueher, *Foundations*, 119–48; Bloomquist, "A Contemporary Exegesis at the Edges of Chaos," *Religion & Theology* 11.1 (2004): 1–38; Bloomquist, "The Rhetoric of Suffering in Paul's

contributed substantively in the area of topos, the incorporation of cognitive science and rhetography into sociorhetorical interpretation, and commentaries on the Gospel of John and 1–3 John during the present decade.[27] During this time, Bloomquist taught a robust curriculum guided by strategies of sociorhetorical analysis and interpretation, and many students produced PhD dissertations either under his supervision or as a result of his teaching and research.[28] The first student

---

Letter to the Philippians: Socio-rhetorical Reflections and Further Thoughts on a Postcolonial Contribution to the Discussion," *Theoforum* 35.2 (2004): 195–223; Bloomquist, "Suffering and Joy: Subverted by Joy in Paul's Letter to the Philippians," *Interpretation* 61.3 (2007): 270–82; Bloomquist, "Rhetoric, Culture, and Ideology: Socio-rhetorical Analysis in the Reading of New Testament Texts," in *Rhetorics in the New Millennium: Promise and Fulfillment*, ed. James D. Hester and J. David Hester, SAC (New York: T&T Clark, 2010), 115–46.

[27] L. Gregory Bloomquist, "The Role of Argumentation in the Miracle Stories of Luke-Acts: Towards a Fuller Identification of Miracle Discourse for Use in Socio-rhetorical Analysis," in *Miracle Discourse in the New Testament*, ed. Duane F. Watson (Atlanta: Society of Biblical Literature, 2012), 85–124; Bloomquist, "The Pesky Threads of Robbins's Rhetorical Tapestry: Vernon K. Robbins's Genealogy of Rhetorical Criticism," in Troy W. Martin, ed., *Genealogies of New Testament Rhetorical Criticism* (Minneapolis: Fortress, 2014), 201–23; Bloomquist, "Visualizing Philippians: Ancient Rhetorical Practice Meets Cognitive Science through Sociorhetorical Interpretation," in *Paul and Ancient Rhetoric: Theory and Practice in the Hellenistic Context*, ed. Stanley E. Porter and Bryan R. Dyer (Cambridge: Cambridge University Press, 2016), 265–84; Bloomquist, "Eyes Wide Open, Seeing Nothing: The Challenge of the Gospel of John's Non-visualizable Texture for Readings Using Visual Texture," in *The Art of Visual Exegesis: Rhetoric, Texts, Images*, ed. Vernon K. Robbins, Walter S. Melion, and Roy R. Jeal, ESEC 19 (Atlanta: SBL Press, 2017), 121–67; Bloomquist, "Methodology for Rhetography and Visual Exegesis of the Gospel of John," in *The Art of Visual Exegesis: Rhetoric, Texts, Images*, ed. Vernon K. Robbins, Walter S. Melion, and Roy R. Jeal, ESEC 19 (Atlanta: SBL Press, 2017), 89–120.

[28] Alexandra Gruca-Macaulay, "A Socio-rhetorical Assessment of Conclusions from the History of Interpretation of the Role of Women in Luke-Acts" (MA thesis, Saint Paul University, Ottawa, 2006); Timothy Beech, "A Socio-rhetorical Analysis of the Development and Function of the Noah-Flood Narrative in *Sibylline Oracles* 1–2" (PhD diss., Saint Paul University, Ottawa, 2007;) François Beyrouti, "Discerning a 'Rhetorics of Catechesis' in Origen of Alexandria's *Commentary on the Gospel of John:* A Sociorhetorical Analysis of Book XIII:3–42 (John 4:13–15)" (PhD diss., Saint Paul University, Ottawa, 2013); Peter Samuel Robinson, "A Sociorhetorical Analysis of Clark H. Pinnock's Hermeneutical Approach to Biblical Materials, with Particular Attention to the Role of Religious Experience" (PhD diss., St. Paul University, Ottawa, 2013); Alexandra Gruca-Macaulay, *Lydia as a Rhetorical Construct in Acts: A Sociorhetorical and Theological Interpretation*, ESEC 18 (Atlanta: SBL Press, 2016), revision of PhD diss., Saint Paul University, Ottawa, 2013; Douglas Finbow, "The Wisdom of the Scribe: A Socio-rhetorical and Theological Interpretation of Sirach 38:24–39:11" (PhD diss., Saint Paul University, 2017); Ben Fung, "Review of *Foundations for Sociorhetorical Exploration,*" *Theoforum* 47.2 (2016–2017):

to complete a PhD dissertation with Bloomquist as advisor was Olu Jerome Megbelayin. Megbelayin was born and raised in a context of Nigerian Yoruba tradition, and as he investigated the Last Supper in Luke 18 he wrestled with relationships and differences between Jewish-based Christian traditions and his own Christian beliefs and practices in the context of polytheistic Yoruba traditions in his home nation of Nigeria.[29] Next was Têtê Délali Gunn's investigation of Paul's travel to Athens and his speaking there, which reverberated with aspects of Gunn's own travel from Togo, West Africa, to Canada, where he engaged in advanced study of the New Testament.[30] Subsequently Gunn was ordained as a minister in the United Church of Canada in 2005, enlisted in the Canadian Armed Forces in 2011, and became a chaplain in his location in Quebec. Currently he serves as course director to the Canadian Forces Chaplain School and Centre at Canadian Forces Base Borden, where he uses sociorhetorical strategies to interpret international religious movements.[31] Priscilla Geisterfer, another Bloomquist student, published a substantive discussion in 1995 of the relation of sociorhetorical interpretation to the feminist criticism of Elisabeth Schüssler Fiorenza.[32] Then a decade later Bloomquist's colleague Normand Bonneau published an essay using narratology to dialogue with the approach to narrational texture in sociorhetorical interpretation.[33] In the meantime, various other dissertations and books that incorporate sociorhetorical strategies of interpretation have emerged in Canada.[34]

Roy R. Jeal, Booth University College, Winnipeg, Canada, began to enter the environment of sociorhetorical interpretation when he participated in the Lund

---

500–502.

[29] Olu Jerome Megbelayin, "A Socio-rhetorical Analysis of the Lukan Narrative of the Last Supper" (PhD diss., Saint Paul University, Ottawa, 2002).

[30] Têtê Délali Gunn, "Prosopopée idéologique de Paul: Une lecture socio-rhétorique du discours de Paul à Athènes: Actes 17,15–18,1)" (PhD diss., Saint Paul University, Ottawa, 2006).

[31] See Éloi Gunn, "Fundamentalist Religious Discourse in Process of Radicalization to Violence—Analysis," *Canadian Military Journal*, 4 May 2018, https://tinyurl.com/SBL3814.

[32] Priscilla Geisterfer, "Full Turns and Half Turns: Engaging the Dialogue/Dance between Elisabeth Schüssler Fiorenza and Vernon Robbins," in *Her Master's Tools? Feminist and Postcolonial Engagements of Historical-Critical Discourse*, ed. Caroline Vander Stichele and Todd Penner, GPBS 9 (Atlanta: Society of Biblical Literature, 2005), 129–44.

[33] Norman Bonneau, "Socio-rhetorical Interpretation's 'Narrational Texture' in Dialogue with Narratology," *Theoforum* 46 (2015), 43–52.

[34] Keir Hammer, "Disambiguating Rebirth: A Socio-rhetorical Exploration of Rebirth Language in 1 Peter" (PhD thesis, University of Toronto, Centre for the Study of Religion, 2011); Harry O. Maier, *Picturing Paul in Empire: Imperial Image, Text and Persuasion in Colossians, Ephesians and the Pastoral Epistles* (London: T&T Clark/Bloomsbury, 2013); Christina Abraham, "The Devil Is in the Details: A Socio-cultural Reading of the Gerasene Narrative in Mark" (MA thesis, Queen's University, Kingston, Ontario, 2016).

2000 and Heidelberg 2002 Pepperdine conferences.[35] This led to a series of essays with special focus on rhetography and rhetorical discourses (rhetorolects),[36] led to his publication of the first Sociorhetorical Exploration Commentary in 2015 in the Rhetoric of Religious Antiquity Series, on Paul's letter to Philemon, and is guiding his preparation of his forthcoming commentary on Colossians.[37]

During the first decade of the twenty-first century, Gerd Theissen gave sociorhetorical lectures at the Chinese University of Hong Kong that appeared as a book, two publications using sociorhetorical interpretation were produced in Norway, and one was produced in Great Britain.[38] Then dissertations and publications

---

[35] Roy R. Jeal, "Rhetorical Argumentation in the Letter to the Ephesians," in *Rhetorical Argumentation in Biblical Texts: Essays from the Lund 2000 Conference*, ed. Anders Eriksson, Thomas H. Olbricht, and Walter Übelacker, ESEC 8 (Harrisburg: Trinity Press International, 2002), 310–24; Jeal, "Melody, Imagery and Memory in the Moral Persuasion of Paul," in *Rhetoric, Ethic and Moral Persuasion in Biblical Discourse*, ed. Thomas H. Olbricht and Anders Eriksson, ESEC 11 (New York: T&T Clark International, 2005), 160–78.

[36] Roy R. Jeal, "Clothes Make the (Wo)Man," *Scriptura* 90 (2005): 685–99, repr., Robbins, von Thaden, and Brueher, *Foundations for Sociorhetorical Explorations*, 393–414; Jeal, "Blending Two Arts: Rhetorical Words, Rhetorical Pictures and Social Formation in the Letter to Philemon," *Sino-Christian Studies* 5 (June 2008): 9–38; Jeal, "Visions of Marriage in Ephesians 5," in *Human Sexuality and the Nuptial Mystery*, ed. Roy R. Jeal (Eugene, OR: Cascade Books, 2010), 116–30; Jeal, "Emerging Christian Discourse: The Acts of Pilate as the Rhetorical Development of Devotion," *Apocrypha* 21 (2010): 151–67; Jeal, "Ideology, Argumentation and Social Direction in Romans 1," in *Human Sexuality and the Nuptial Mystery*, ed. Roy R. Jeal (Eugene OR: Cascade Books, 2010), 27–44; Jeal, "Starting before the Beginning: Precreation Discourse in Colossians," *Religion and Theology* 18.1–2 (2011): 287–310; "Sociorhetorical Intertexture," in *Exploring Intertextuality: Diverse Strategies for New Testament Interpretation of Texts*, ed. B. J. Oropeza and Steve Moyise (Eugene, OR: Cascade Books, 2016), 151–64; Jeal, "Visual Exegesis: Blending Rhetorical Arts in Colossians 2:6–3:4," in *The Art of Visual Exegesis: Rhetoric; Texts; Images*, ed. Vernon K. Robbins, Walter S. Melion, and Roy R. Jeal, ESEC 19 (Atlanta: SBL Press, 2017), 55–87.

[37] Roy R. Jeal, *Exploring Philemon: Freedom, Brotherhood, and Partnership in the New Society*, RRA 2 (Atlanta: SBL Press, 2015); Jeal, *Exploring Colossians: Transferred to the New Reality*, RRA (Atlanta: SBL Press, forthcoming).

[38] Gerd Theissen, *Gospel Writing and Church Politics: A Socio-rhetorical Approach*, Chuen King Lecture Series 3 (Hong Kong: Theology Division, Chung Chi College, Chinese University of Hong Kong, 2001); Marianne Bjelland Kartzow, *Gossip and Gender: Othering of Speech in the Pastoral Epistles*, BZNW 164 (Berlin: de Gruyter, 2009); revision of ThD diss., University of Oslo, Norway, 2007; Ingeborg A. K. Kvammen, *Toward a Postcolonial Reading of the Epistle of James: James 2:1–13 in its Roman Imperial Context*, BINS 119 (Leiden: Brill, 2013), revision of PhD Thesis, School of Mission and Theology, Stavanger, Norway, 2008; David H. Wenkel, *Joy in Luke-Acts: The Intersection of Rhetoric, Narrative, and Emotion*, Paternoster Biblical Monographs Series (Crownhill, UK: Paternoster, 2015), revision of PhD diss., University of Aberdeen, UK, 2011.

began to appear in India,[39] then in Hong Kong and Indonesia.[40] Also Gerson Mgaya, student of Kidugala Lutheran Seminary, Tanzania, and University of Eastern Finland, Kuopio, published his ThD dissertation on spiritual gifts in 1 Cor 12–14 in 2016.[41]

During the first two decades of the twenty-first century, dissertations and publications incorporating sociorhetorical interpretation began to appear in New Zealand and Australia.[42] Completing his MTh thesis at the University of Auckland, New Zealand, under the guidance of Professor Elaine Wainwright, Vaitusi Nofoaiga began introducing sociorhetorical interpretation to Malua Theological

---

[39] Santosh V. Varghese, "Woe-Oracles in Habakkuk 2:6–20: A Socio-rhetorical Reading" (MTh thesis, Faith Theological Seminary, Manakala, Kerala, India, 2009); Cyprian E. Fernandez, *Identity in Conflict: A Socio-rhetorical Reading of the Markan Story of Jesus* (Bengaluru, India: Asian Trading Corporation, 2016); Sebastian Victor Antonyraj, "The Centurion, A Transformational Leader: A Socio-Rhetorical Analysis of Matthew 8,5–13," (PhD diss., Pontifical University of Saint Thomas Aquinas, Rome, 2017); Chubamongba Ao, "'In all the Work of Your Hands' in Deuteronomy: An Inquiry on Rhetoric of Work" (DTh diss., South Asia Theological Research Institute, Union Biblical Seminary, Pune, Maharashtra, India, 2017); N. Subramani, "Imagery of Love as a Paradigm for Covenantal Relationship in the Book of Hosea: A Socio-Rhetorical Reading" (DTh diss., South Asia Theological Research Institute, Union Biblical Seminary, Pune, Maharashtra, India, 2018); George P. Seb, "A Socio-rhetorical Analysis of YHWH's Speeches in Selected Texts of Exodus 2–11 with Focus on Redemption and the Knowledge of YHWH" (DTh diss., United Theological College, Bangalore, India, forthcoming); Vincilo G. Shaaber, "Revisiting the Addressees of the Apocalypse: A Socio-rhetorical Reading of Revelation 13" (MTh thesis, United Theological College, Bangalore, India, forthcoming).

[40] Alex Hon Ho Ip, *A Socio-rhetorical Interpretation of the Letter to Philemon in Light of the New Institutional Economics: An Exhortation to Transform a Master-Slave Economic Relationship into a Brotherly Loving Relationship*, WUNT 2/444 (Tübingen: Mohr Siebeck, 2017), revision of PhD diss., The Chinese University of Hong Kong, 2014; Rospita Deliana Siahaan, "Speaking in Tongues in Public Worship? A Socio-Rhetorical Approach to 1 Corinthians 12–14" (PhD diss., Lutheran Theological Seminary, Shatin, Hong Kong, 2015), published in Indonesian translation as *Bahasa Roh Dalam Ibadah Jemaat? Tafsir Sosio-Retorika 1 Korintus 12–14* (Jakarta: BPK-GM), 2017.

[41] Gerson Mgaya, *Spiritual Gifts: A Sociorhetorical Interpretation of 1 Cor 12–14* (Amazon, 2017).

[42] Kayle B. de Waal, *A Socio-rhetorical Interpretation of the Seven Trumpets of Revelation: The Apocalyptic Challenge to Earthly Empire* (Lewiston, NY: Edwin Mellen, 2012), revision of PhD diss., University of Auckland, New Zealand, 2010; Rosemary Canavan, *Clothing the Body of Christ at Colossae: A Visual Construction of Identity*, WUNT 2/334 (Tübingen: Mohr Siebeck, 2012), revision of PhD diss., Flinders University, South Australia, 2011; Nina Corlett-MacDonald, "Jesus and 'Other' Deviants: A Narrative Labelling Study of 'Aloneness' in Mark 5:1–20" (PhD diss., Flinders University, South Australia, 2016).

College, Samoa, in 2007.[43] During the first four years when Nofoaiga was a lecturer at Malua Theological College, Caesar Samuelu and Perenise Malota completed BD theses using sociorhetorical interpretation.[44] Then Seumaninoa Puaina completed his BD thesis on Jesus's feeding of the five thousand in 2012, attained his PhD at the Graduate Theological Union, Berkeley, California, in 2016, and now is a lecturer at Malua Theological College.[45] Then Nofoaiga completed his PhD at the University of Auckland, which has recently been published in the SBL International Voices in Biblical Studies series.[46] This publication has set a standard for using sociorhetorical interpretation to integrate Samoan language, society, institutions, and culture into biblical interpretation. Also during this time, Nofoaiga has published a series of essays using sociorhetorical interpretation to interpret other passages in the New Testament.[47] Currently, Nofoaiga has in preparation an essay on "The Gracious Torah in the Gospel of Matthew" for *Testamentum Imperium* online and a book in Samoan on a sociorhetorical reading of the Book of Revelation from a Samoan perspective. From 2015 to 2019 twelve students, nurtured by the teaching and supervision of Nofoaiga, have used sociorhetorical interpretation for BTh, BD, or BD with Honors, or MTh theses.[48] In

---

[43] Vaitusi Nofoaiga, "Crowds as Jesus' Disciples in the Matthean Gospel" (MTh thesis, University of Auckland, New Zealand, 2007).

[44] Caesar Samuelu, "Head Covering for Women in 1 Corinthians 11:2–16" (BD thesis, Malua Theological College, Samoa, 2008); Perenise Malota, "What Jesus Said about Divorce: A Samoan Christian Biblical Interpretation of Matthew 19:1–9" (BD thesis, Malua Theological College, Samoa, 2010).

[45] Seumaninoa Puaina, "The Feeding of the 5000 (Matthew 14:13–20): A New Missionary Paradigm for the Congregational Church Samoa" (BD thesis, Malua Theological College, Samoa, 2011); Puaina, "Beyond Universalism: Unraveling the Anonymous Minor Characters in Matthew 15:21–28" (PhD diss., Graduate Theological Union, Berkeley, California, 2016).

[46] Vaitusi Nofoaiga, *A Samoan Reading of Discipleship in Matthew*, IVBS 8 (Atlanta: SBL Press, 2017), revision of Nofoaiga, "Towards a Samoan Postcolonial Reading of Discipleship in Matthew's Gospel" (PhD diss., University of Auckland, New Zealand, 2014).

[47] Vaitusi Nofoaiga, "Exploring Discipleship in Matthew 4:12–25 from *tautuaileva* (Service/servant/serve in Between)," *Pacific Journal of Theology* 50 (2013): 61–87; Nofoaiga, "Jesus the *Fiaola* (Opportunity Seeker): A Postcolonial Samoan Reading of Matthew 7:24–8:22," in *Sea of Readings: The Bible in the South Pacific*, ed. Jione Havea, Semeia Studies 90 (Atlanta: SBL Press, 2018), 163–77; Nofoaiga, "A Samoan Reading of Judas's Betrayal of Jesus," in *Point of View Publishing: Customized Course Readings*, ed. Mark Roncace and Joseph Weaver, Religion, Biblical Studies (2018), https://tinyurl.com/SBL3814a.

[48] Tieem Meetari, "An Interpretation of Giving Gifts in 2 Corinthians 9:1–15 from a Kiribati Perspective" (BD thesis, Malua Theological College, Samoa, 2015); Fatilua Fatilua, "The Church and Court Litigation: A Socio-rhetorical Analysis of 1 Corinthians 6:1–11" (BD thesis, Malua Theological College, Samoa, 2016); Fatilua, *Fāiā Analysis of Romans 13:1–17: Integrating A Samoan Perspective with Socio-rhetorical Criticism* (MTh thesis,

addition, Elekosi Lafitaga has produced a PhD dissertation using sociorhetorical strategies to interpret metaphorical dimensions of the Animal Apocalypse in 1 Enoch in relation to apocalyptic discourse in the Gospel of Matthew at the Graduate Theological Union, Berkeley, California.[49]

For me, the international emergence of sociorhetorical interpretation has been far beyond anything imagined during my boyhood on that little farm outside Ithaca, Nebraska. Starting with a Fulbright Fellowship in 1983–1984 at the University of Trondheim, Norway, sponsored by Professor Peder Borgen, which included lectures in Great Britain and Scotland, I began to experience the joy and growth of prolonged relationships with scholars in other parts of the world. In the midst of the expansion of these experiences throughout Europe and all the Scandinavian countries including Iceland, the invitation to give lectures and workshops throughout South Africa in 1996 opened the door for experiences truly beyond my wildest dreams. Through generous hosting, planning, and invitation, Professor H. J. Bernard Combrink inaugurated and sustained a Visiting Professorship at the University of Stellenbosch from 1999–2004. During this time period, many scholars and their families and friends welcomed me and my wife Deanna at multiple universities throughout South Africa. Faculty at UNISA in Pretoria arranged a prolonged tour of Kruger National Park, and, at an extended visit at the University

---

Pacific Theological College, Suva, Fiji, 2018); Timoteo Tapelu, "*Tautua* as a Hermeneutical Tool to Understand Paul's View of Justification by Faith in 2 Corinthians 9:6–15 and the EFKS Ministry" (BD thesis, Malua Theological College, Samoa, 2016); Latu Afioga, "A *Tuagane* (Brother to a Sister) Reading of Jesus' Conversation with the Syrophoenician Woman in Mark 7:24–30" (BD thesis, Malua Theological College, Samoa, 2016); Kuresa Tavalani, "Jesus' Encounter with the Samaritan Woman (John 4:16–30) from *Tuagane* (Brother to a Sister) Perspective" (BTh thesis, Malua Theological College, 2016); Clarke Stowers, "Names as Hermeneutics to Read Texts: *Fofogaolevai* and John the Baptizer (Mark 1:1–15)" (BTh thesis, Malua Theological College, Samoa, 2017); Faamoana Leaupepe, "The Widow's Offering: A Socio-rhetorical Reading of Mark 12:41–44" (Malua Theological College, Samoa, 2017); Faalefu Tumutalie, "Re-reading Matthew 22:15–22 Amid a Taxation Law Affecting Church Ministers in Samoa" (BTh thesis, Malua Theological College, Samoa, 2018); Leuelu Setu, "Revisiting Judas's Betrayal of Jesus in the Gospel of Matthew 26:14–16, 45–47; 27:3–10, (BD with Honor thesis, Malua Theological College, Samoa, 2018); Kaititi Tokaia, "A Kiribati Reading of the Wedding Feast in Matthew 22:1–14" (BD with Honors thesis, Malua Theological College, Samoa 2019); Challis Pupi, "A Samoan Reading of Jesus' True Family in Matthew 12:45–50" (BTh thesis, Malua Theological College, Samoa 2019); Isoa Cailala Vatanitawake, "*Tuirara*, The Standing One: A Sociorhetorical Reading of Acts 6:1–7 in the Context of *Tuirara—Talatala* Relationship in the Methodist Church in Fiji" (MTh thesis, Pacific Theological College, Suva, Fiji, 2019).

[49] Elekosi F. Lafitaga, "Apocalyptic, Here and Now: The Book of Dreams (1 Enoch 83–90) and the Rhetoric of Apocalyptic Discourse in the Gospel of Matthew" (PhD diss., Graduate Theological Union, Berkeley, California, 2017).

of KwaZulu-Natal, Professor J. A. Bobby Loubser and his wife Minnie arranged special experiences of the surrounding area. Since those experiences, special times in Canada and Europe, and visits by scholars from Australia, Indonesia, China, India, Denmark, Iceland, Samoa, Fiji, and Norway have provided treasured moments of international understanding and exchange. It is exciting to think what the future may bring as a result of new and renewing friendships that continue year by year.

Strengths and Gaps of Foundations for Sociorhetorical Exploration

Shively T. J. Smith

Writers are among the most sensitive, the most intellectually anarchic, most representative, most probing of artists. The ability of writers to imagine what is not the self, to familiarize the strange and mystify the familiar, is the test of their power. The language they use and the social and historical context in which these languages signify are indirect and direct revelations of that power and its limitations.[1]

In her book, *Playing in the Dark*, American novelist and Pulitzer Prize winner Toni Morrison reflects on the creative processes of writers "and the route imagination takes when it is shaped by cultural and social forces" that can cultivate or impede freedom of exploration, discovery, representation, rhetorical invention, and impact.[2] Although the focus of the quotation above from Morrison is the history of the American literary imagination shaped by racial realities, her statement can also serve as a useful frame for considering the strengths and gaps of the 2016 edited volume, *Foundations for Sociorhetorical Exploration: A Rhetoric of Religious Antiquity Reader*.[3] Indeed, like Morrison's ideal image of literary writers, *Foundations for Sociorhetorical Exploration* demonstrates the ability of a group of biblical interpreters to imagine other angles for exploring and describing the religious rhetoric of early Christian texts within its larger literary and social-historical environments of the Hellenistic Jewish and Greco-

---

[1] Toni Morrison, *Playing in the Dark: Whiteness and the Literary Imagination* (Cambridge, MA: Harvard University Press, 1992), 15.
[2] Michael Eric Dyson, *Reflecting Black: African-American Cultural Criticism* (Minneapolis: University of Minnesota, 1993), 179–80.
[3] Vernon K. Robbins, Robert H. von Thaden Jr., and Bart B. Bruehler, eds., *Foundations for Sociorhetorical Exploration: A Rhetoric of Religious Antiquity Reader*, RRA 4 (Atlanta: SBL Press, 2016).

Roman worlds. *Foundations for Sociorhetorical Exploration* embodies some of the manifold practices of *interpretive play* in sociorhetorical interpretation (SRI) that bring the resources of imagination and attention to texts as rhetorical productions with an unlimited meaning potential. Such an interpretive orientation can be labeled strange even as it accomplishes repeatedly the difficult task of mystifying familiar early Christian texts. Perhaps the same should be said about this collective of sociorhetorical practitioners who focus on early Christian texts and discourses as about Morrison's literary writers for both "are among the most sensitive, the most intellectually anarchic, most representative, most probing of artists."[4]

In the history of sociorhetorical interpretation, *Foundations for Sociorhetorical Exploration* stands as the anniversary text, archiving some of the important programmatic developments in SRI since its 1996 classic explication in two books by Vernon Robbins called, *The Tapestry of Early Christian Discourse* and *Exploring the Texture of Texts*.[5] Twelve essays are divided among five major sections representing ever-flowing streams of literary and historical, social and ideological, symbolic and semantic explorations of evolving Mediterranean religious discourses. As the introduction in *Foundations for Sociorhetorical Exploration* states, "certain articles have come to stand out as formative influences, ongoing dialogue partners, and crucial steps forward in the expansion of the [sociorhetorical] analytic."[6] In this description of the project, newcomers to SRI hear hints of the abiding commitment among its practitioners to explore and elaborate the analytic as new voices, perspectives, resources, and curiosities present themselves. This is no coincidence. As one of its contributors says, "Sociorhetorical analysis is very much an approach that is in the *process* of being shaped."[7]

Moreover, the opening comments in the volume trace the development and spread of SRI in terms of its approach and appropriation. Indeed, it is these two tenets—approach and appropriation—that the edited volume embodies and to which this review attends while naming some strengths and gaps in the showcase of SRI's programmatic development. This review does not address every essay included in the volume; each is rich with new insights and new interpretive trajectories in its own way. Rather, this review describes several strengths

---

[4] Morrison, *Playing in the Dark*, 15.
[5] Vernon K. Robbins, *The Tapestry of Early Christian Discourse: Rhetoric, Society and Ideology* (London: Routledge, 1996); Robbins, *Exploring the Texture of Texts: A Guide to Socio-rhetorical Interpretation* (Valley Forge, PA: Trinity Press International, 1996).
[6] Robbins, von Thaden, and Bruehler, introduction to *Foundations for Sociorhetorical Exploration*, 7.
[7] L. Gregory Bloomquist, "Paul's Inclusive Language: The Ideological Texture of Romans 1," in Robbins, von Thaden, and Bruehler, *Foundations for Sociorhetorical Exploration*, 119.

and one significant gap in the work, mentioning some essays as representative, with the hope that no false impression is left that other essays in the volume do not also exhibit those characteristics. Certainly an overarching and commendable strength of *Foundations for Sociorhetorical Exploration* is that the story of SRI's evolution as a collaborative interpretive endeavor is laid bare for all to see. Moreover, the collection demonstrates the broad swath of cross-disciplinary approaches SRI brings to the task of analyzing the rhetoric of ancient Christian writings and the diversity of scholarly interests and curiosities to which SRI lends itself.

Strengths of *Foundations for Sociorhetorical Exploration*

One of the strengths of the volume is the way it repeatedly defines what it is in contrast to what it is not. For example, the volume opens with the following declaration:

> Sociorhetorical interpretation (SRI) is a heuristic that is properly called an interpretive analytic rather than a method. This means an interpreter can select any series of strategies to analyze and interpret rhetorical, social, and cognitive picturing and reasoning to help interpreters learn how a text prompts and influences thinking, emotion, and behavior. Since it is not a method, it does not prescribe a series of scientific steps or formulae designed to perform and produce predictable results in accord with a particular conceptual framework.[8]

Just by reading the opening pages of the volume, readers learn what to expect in the collection—namely, a demonstration of the experiential nature of SRI rather than a linear, methodical sequencing of steps. Throughout the book, the essays demonstrate multiple entryways into SRI without asserting any one approach as greater than others. For instance, L. Gregory Bloomquist opens his essay "Paul's Inclusive Language: The Ideological Texture of Romans 1" by asserting that SRI eschews methodological hegemony in favor of a more healthy and inclusion-based model. Bloomquist insists that SRI "welcomes all voices to the table, without deciding in a priori fashion that only some voices will be heard."[9] Consequently, it appears SRI offers a variety of angles by which to engage, probe, and understand the early Christian texts without asserting one angle or texture of the text is more valuable than another.

Moreover, newcomers learn from *Foundations for Sociorhetorical Exploration* that SRI brings together "rhetorical, sociological, and anthropological strategies into literary-historical exegesis of early Christian literature."[10] As

---

[8] Robbins, von Thaden, and Bruehler, introduction to *Foundations for Sociorhetorical Exploration*, 1.
[9] Bloomquist, "Paul's Inclusive Language," 119.
[10] Robbins, von Thaden, and Bruehler, introduction to *Foundations for Sociorhetorical*

such, the approach acknowledges explicitly the multi-dimensional nature of religious discourse in its origin, but also in its intention and impact. By recognizing how language is wielded to persuade hearers and readers, SRI challenges notions of neutral interpretation while searching for and describing the way language is socially, politically, and culturally embedded as well as historically informed. Hence, *Foundations for Sociorhetorical Exploration* expands the reading strategies available to work with texts and, in turn, expands the landscape of meaning potential of discourses and narratives.

Another strength of the volume is the way each essay offers a full picture of the nature and function of its particular focus within the larger sociorhetorical enterprise. The contributors, to varying degrees, demonstrate how they have expanded the hermeneutical and theoretical grounding of the sociorhetorical analytic beyond dominant Western canons in the history of interpretation by incorporating theories and findings from other cross-disciplinary fields— especially cognitive sciences, cultural anthropology, linguistics, spatial studies, and ideological criticism, to name a few. The essays never disappoint in this regard. Each rehearses a history of scholarship and/or a history of terms, which offer readers the opportunity to build their own bibliography for future research. Such a strategy is intentional, as the contributors make clear that in order to develop the particular concepts and approaches their essays exhibit, pre-existent intellectual resources first must be identified and reconfigured in new ways. For instance, in his programmatic essay, "Sociorhetorical Criticism: Mary, Elizabeth, and the Magnificat as a Test Case," Robbins says, "The beginnings of Sociorhetorical criticism lie in the goals for biblical interpretation Amos N. Wilder set forth in his presidential address to the Society of Biblical Literature in 1955 entitled, 'Scholars, Theologians, and Ancient Rhetoric.'"[11] In addition to Wilder, SRI identifies the works of scholars like Wayne A. Meeks, Jonathan Z. Smith, Wilhelm Wuellner, and Elisabeth Schüssler Fiorenza as contributing to the "generative interdisciplinary work" flourishing in the classic formulation of SRI's five-textured approach.[12] The five textures of texts that SRI explores are called inner texture, intertexture, social and culture texture, ideological texture, and sacred texture. Each represents a different entryway to the sociorhetorical reading strategy overall and serves as the basis of SRI's appreciation for diversity, multidimensionality, and flexibility.

In addition to rehearsing the history of scholarship and/or history of terms contributing to the classic formulation of SRI, the essays carve out new pathways in SRI and review the history of scholarship related to that new lens. For

---

Exploration, 2.

[11] Robbins, "Sociorhetorical Criticism: Mary, Elizabeth, and the Magnificat as a Test Case," in *Foundations for Sociorhetorical Exploration*, 31.

[12] Robbins, von Thaden, and Bruehler, introduction to *Foundations for Sociorhetorical Exploration*, 8.

instance, in talking about "Theories of Space and Construction of the Ancient World," Jon L. Berquist acknowledges the relatively young discourse on the study of space as genealogical and historical discourse. He says, "In the last thirty-five years, culture as a whole and philosophy in particular have granted increasing attention to space. Current literature on space routinely nods to Michel Foucault's 1967 lecture, "Of Other Spaces," as the first time that space began to have a history, or at least a possibility for a history."[13] Berquist goes on to expand his list of theoreticians on space to include scholars such as Werner Heisenberg and Edward Soja. Berquist sketches some of the positions he deems pertinent for a sociorhetorical investigation and use of space as a historical interpretative site. Similarly, Lynn R. Huber brings a full-bodied understanding of metaphor to the SRI analytic by exploring various scholarly discussions on it from the context of ancient rhetoric, the Middle Ages, and contemporary literary criticism. She goes on to elucidate a richly textured understanding of metaphor by attending to the metaphors in the book of Revelation. Huber names and explores Aristotle's body of work on metaphor (*Poetics*, *Rhetoric*, etc.) as well as the works on metaphor by Latin rhetoricians such as Cicero, the *Rhetorica ad Herennium*, Quintilian, and Augustine, demonstrating the rhetorical underpinning and center of SRI exploration.[14]

In sum, a noteworthy strength of *Foundations for Sociorhetorical Exploration* is how consistently the contributors reinforce the importance of the classic 1996 SRI formulation, even as they nudge the analytic in new directions. For example, Robert von Thaden in his essay says, "Any means to investigate the production and understanding of meaning by humanity must simply take into account the fact that humans are embodied, social agents. This is a point upon which cognitive scientists and Sociorhetorical interpreters agree and which demonstrates the usefulness of cognitive science approach to religion within a Sociorhetorical framework."[15] Von Thaden's description exemplifies how each contribution both affirms and expands SRI's modes of interpretation. What emerges from such fresh articulations of SRI are endeavors to escape a linear process of interpretation. Each essay demonstrates how SRI functions as a sort of crossway where multiple interpretive strategies, interests, approaches, and resources meet "to discover the rhetoric of *topoi*, pictures, textures, and emer-

---

[13] Jon L. Berquist, "Theories of Space and Construction of the Ancient World," in Robbins, von Thaden, and Bruehler, *Foundations for Sociorhetorical Exploration*, 151.

[14] Lynn R. Huber, "Knowing Is Seeing: Theories of Metaphor Ancient, Medieval, and Modern," in Robbins, von Thaden, and Bruehler, *Foundations for Sociorhetorical Exploration*, 236–40.

[15] Robert H. von Thaden Jr., "A Cognitive Turn: Conceptual Blending within a Sociorhetorical Framework," in Robbins, von Thaden, and Bruehler, *Foundations for Sociorhetorical Exploration*, 287.

gent structures that texts prompt in the minds of hearers and readers in ways that form and reform them socially and religiously."[16]

Finding a Gap in *Foundations for Sociorhetorical Exploration* and Its Significance for Sociorhetorical Interpretation

The open entryways and, thus, undefined endpoints of sociorhetorical interpretation make it difficult to identify a gap in its analytic. After all, the classic explication of SRI's theoretical underpinnings and goals set out in *The Tapestry of Early Christian Discourse,* which persists among the contributors of *Foundations for Sociorhetorical Exploration,* is "to generate multiple, conscious strategies for reading and rereading texts in an integrated environment of interpretation." Robbins asserts that, "The goal is not so much to attain agreement among interpreters as to nurture cooperation in the gathering, analysis and interpretation of data, even among people who disagree with one another."[17] In an interpretive environment that welcomes—even requires—plurality of strategies while embracing disagreement as an inevitable state of affairs, it is difficult to name a gap the analytic leaves open because opportunities abound for something not being done in the reading strategies to be taken up and engaged.

As noted above, Gregory Bloomquist asserts that one of SRI's strengths is that it eschews methodological hegemony while favoring multiple, interdisciplinary methodological approaches.[18] In addition to embracing methodological plurality, Bloomquist describes SRI as seeking "to find the stuff of real people in texts that are so often relegated to a merely textual world or, more and more today, are reduced to texts that 'evidence' not real people but what can only be called 'stick figures.'"[19] Undoubtedly, the attempt to find "the stuff of real people in texts" is a laudable strength, but herein may also reside a growing area in SRI's representative work. Although hints of attending to "the stuff of real people in texts" are present in the volume, certain aspects remain undeveloped and lack "thick description," to take a term from one of the cultural anthropologists central to SRI, Clifford Geertz.

As stated earlier, SRI incorporates rhetorical, sociological, and anthropological strategies into literary-historical exegesis. However, one inchoate dimension of SRI's current appropriation is its limited definition and use of what it considers anthropological and sociological resources for understanding the rhetorical nature of specific religious texts and its reverberating influences throughout his-

---

[16] Robbins, von Thaden, and Bruehler, introduction to *Foundations for Sociorhetorical Exploration*, 1.
[17] Robbins, von Thaden, and Bruehler, introduction to *Foundations for Sociorhetorical Exploration*, 3.
[18] Bloomquist, "Paul's Inclusive Language," 119.
[19] Bloomquist, "Paul's Inclusive Language," 119.

tory. This is particularly glaring in regard to SRI's focus on the rhetorical force of texts as "emergent discourse." Sociorhetorical interpretation defines the rhetorical force of early Christian texts as "The emerging discourse of a social, cultural, ideological, and/or religious movement like early Christianity as it participated in reconfigurations of belief, behavior, and community formation in the Mediterranean world."[20] One way to gain a strong sense of the rhetorical impact and significance of respective texts in its early interpretive life is to pay attention to how the writings faired in later Christian contexts that share similarities in terms of social, cultural, and ideological characteristics. This represents a slightly different approach to using resources like sociological and anthropological models. Indeed, this is not an entirely new idea to practitioners of SRI. For example, almost from its beginning, SRI recognized the importance of John Gager's 1975 groundbreaking text *Kingdom and Community*, in which modern sociological and social scientific models were employed to interpret ancient Christian texts and generate new social-historical data.[21] Gager's work of bringing more contemporary experiences and contexts to bear in appreciating the early Christian contexts and literature was instructive. Contributors to *Foundations for Sociorhetorical Exploration* acknowledge the essential step of establishing contextual conversations between ancient and contemporary worlds and name it an area that needs to be taken up and developed further in the work of SRI.[22]

Although the volume provides a glimpse of how distinct, yet similar, social and ideological contexts in time, space, and language can be conversant within the cadre of SRI strategies, it remains undeveloped. No full essay of such an approach is included in the volume. One example, however, is referenced in a list of dissertations that have used SRI strategies. Miranda Pillay's dissertation from the University of Western Cape, "Re-visioning Stigma: A Socio-rhetorical Reading of Luke 10:25–37 in the Context of HIV/AIDS in South Africa," uses SRI to cultivate a conversation between an early Christian discourse and a con-

---

[20] Robbins, von Thaden, and Bruehler, *Foundations for Sociorhetorical Exploration*, xxii.
[21] John G. Gager, *Kingdom and Community: The Social World of Early Christianity* (Englewood Cliffs NJ: Prentice Hall, 1975), noted in Robbins, von Thaden, and Bruehler, *Foundations for Sociorhetorical Exploration*, 4, 35–36, 127, n.29.
[22] Vernon K. Robbins, "Socio-rhetorical Criticism: Mary, Elizabeth, and the Magnificat as a Test Case," in Robbins, von Thaden, and Bruehler, *Foundations for Sociorhetorical Exploration*, 35. Robbins makes such statement in his 1994 essay included in *Foundations for Sociorhetorical Exploration*, by saying, "the task of incorporating the insights of this paradigm programmatically into exegesis of New Testament texts still lies in the future. Sociorhetorical criticism sets forth a programmatic set of strategies to pursue, test, enrich, and revise the provisional conclusions Gager advances in his book" (Robbins, "Socio-rhetorical Criticism," 36).

temporary crisis.[23] She argues that while the challenges presented by the AIDS pandemic are scientific and medical, it also has other impacts on those infected and affected (psychological, legal, economic, social, ethical and religious), that require the church to develop a multi-disciplinary response. Her work explores Luke's Gospel as "a resource for shaping the church's response." Pillay demonstrates that by using SRI, Luke's Gospel becomes a resource for contemporary conversations and issues even as SRI provides interpretive pathways for navigating the hermeneutical challenges of deploying a first century document in the twenty-first century societal context. As she says, "Besides the historical gap (with all its social and cultural ramifications), New Testament texts lend itself to diverse, contradictory and ambiguous interpretations." Yet, SRI offers a way of bridging the historical gap and managing the hermeneutical conundrum.

Likewise, Bloomquist supposes there is the opportunity to use SRI strategies for bridging the historical gap between the social and cultural concerns of ancient New Testament texts with the concerns of the present day. He concludes his essay with a provocative paragraph in which he alludes to such an appropriation being on the horizon. He says:

> If we want to do more than understand, if we want to enter this world and see for ourselves what Paul saw and what he sought to reconfigure, then we need to enter worlds that are shaped by how far ethnic hatred can go, since ethnic hatred is simply the extension of self-gratifying views that 'we' are perfect judges and that 'the other' is both God's enemy and ours, whether 'the other' is gentile or Jew, male or female, slave or free, barbarian or Greek, Parthian or Roman, white or black, Hutu or Tutsi, Israeli or Palestinian, Serb or Kosovar. Thus perhaps we will get the full impact of the situation Paul is talking about and why that reconfiguration was so important to him only when we see the images from Rwanda, from Israel, from Indonesia, and from India and recognize in them the face of ethnic hatred, the hatred of one who is not family.[24]

In a global world at odds with itself because of ethnic discord, ever-growing suspicion of strangers, xenophobia, unstable ecological systems, uneven distributions of global wealth, limited healthcare access, and ongoing failures to provide the basic needs necessary to ensure all humans can live in dignity and flourish, SRI has a unique opportunity. As both Pillay and Bloomquist suggest, SRI can deploy its analytic as a way to construct another conversation—namely, one that interacts with both the environments of early Christian texts and the contemporary contexts from which SRI practitioners do their work. Forging a way to live in both sociorhetorical worlds—the worlds of the past and the pre-

---

[23] Miranda Pillay, "Re-visioning Stigma: A Socio-rhetorical Reading of Luke 10:25–37 in the Context of HIV/AIDS in South Africa" (PhD diss., University of the Western Cape, South Africa, 2008).

[24] Bloomquist, "Paul's Inclusive Language," 148.

sent—is a challenge SRI has the capacity to address more intentionally in its future evolution.

Conclusion

Although *Foundations for Sociorhetorical Exploration* leaves open a critical gap or area of opportunity for future work, there should be no lack of respect and appreciation for the diverse approaches and appropriations represented in the volume. The very programmatic characteristics of SRI argue for the evolution of its practice, deployment, and implementation. Its own interpretive and intellectual artifacts as exhibited in *Foundations for Sociorhetorical Exploration* show a genuine embrace of development and expansion in practice, perspective, and engagement with ancient texts be they early Christian, Jewish, non-Semitic Mediterranean texts, and so forth. That SRI shows signs of this process of expansion in its interpretive history is not just a contextual curiosity but also an aspect of the nature of the SRI approach, as its practitioners understand it. One hopes that interpreters deploying SRI will continue to expand their gazes, being informed by and inclusive of the rhetorical forces of early Christian texts when wielded in contexts beyond early Christianity, embodying fidelity to the spirit of the approach in which SRI was created and to which the practitioners of SRI began to take up their work.

In conclusion, it is prudent to return where this review started, with Toni Morrison's words. In another famous quotation from Morrison about the writer's task, she says, "If there is a book that you want to read, but it hasn't been written yet, you must be the one to write it." The practitioners of SRI included in *Foundations for Sociorhetorical Exploration* can be indicted for *or* applauded for one charge: There were and are a variety of ways to read ancient Christian texts that have not been done yet, and each one decided she or he was one of the persons to do just that—read texts in new ways. It is for this reason that their efforts should be celebrated.

Part 2
Explorations in Australia and Oceania

An Australian Ecological Engagement with Sociorhetorical Interpretation

Michael Trainor

Introduction: The Global and Environmental Context

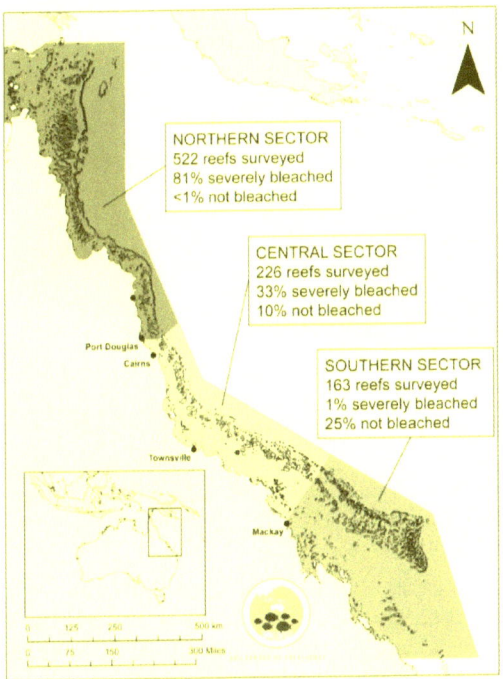

The largest living organism in the southern hemisphere is located just off the northeast coast of Australia. The "Great Barrier Reef," as we name it, is the world's most extensive living ecosystem. Nearly three thousand individual coral systems and one thousand islands compose this reef, one of the great natural wonders of the planet. Coral bleaching, ocean warming and acidification, the explosion in population of the crown-of-thorns starfish, and other environmental issues have seriously damaged the reef. A 2012 study by researchers of the Australian Institute of Marine Science suggests that since 1985 half

Fig. 1. Map of the Great Barrier Reef showing results of aerial surveys for 911 reefs. Courtesy of ARC Centre of Excellence for Coral Reef Studies/Tom Bridge and James Kerry.

of the reef's cover has disappeared and 93 percent of it affected by coral bleaching.[1]

The effects of climate change reflected in the Great Barrier Reef is a microcosm of what is happening globally. We are aware of local situations, bushfires, floods, increased average temperatures, and the diminishment of Arctic ice.

According to the 2015 synthesis report of the *Intergovernmental Panel on Climate Change (IPPC)*,

> Human influence on the climate system is clear, and recent anthropogenic emissions of greenhouse gases are the highest in history. Recent climate changes have had widespread impacts on human and natural systems…. Warming of the climate system is unequivocal, and since the 1950s, many of the observed changes are unprecedented over decades to millennia. The atmosphere and ocean have warmed, the amounts of snow and ice have diminished, and sea level has risen.[2]

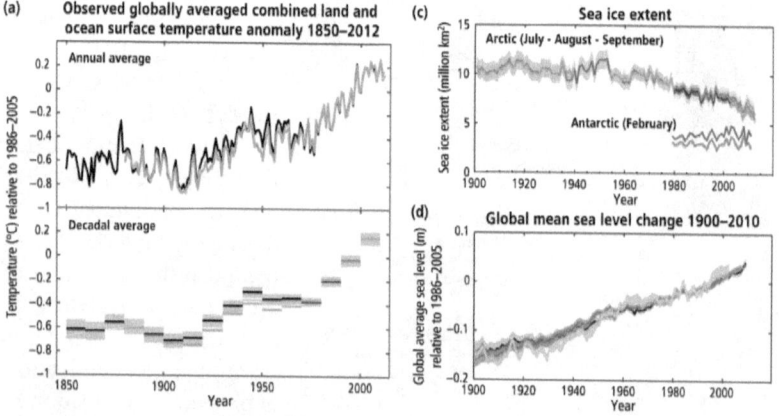

Fig. 2. IPPC observations and summary of land and ocean temperature, sea level change and sea ice extent. IPCC, *Fifth Assessment Report: Climate Change 2014*.

---

[1] Juliet Eilperin, "Great Barrier Reef Has Lost Half Its Coral Since 1985 New Study Says," *The Washington Post*, 1 October 2012. Fig. 1 credit: "Only 7% of the Great Barrier Reef Has Avoided Coral Bleaching," https://www.coralcoe.org.au/media-releases/only-7-of-the-great-barrier-reef-has-avoided-coral-bleaching.

[2] IPCC, *Fifth Assessment Report: Climate Change 2014*, https://www.ipcc.ch/pdf/assessment-report/ar5, p. 41. Figure 2 credit: Figure 1.1 from Observed Changes and their Causes. IPCC, 2014: *Climate Change 2014: Synthesis Report. Contribution of Working Groups I, II and III to the Fifth Assessment Report of the Intergovernmental Panel on Climate Change.* Core Writing Team, ed. R. K. Pachauri and L. A. Meyer. IPCC, Geneva, Switzerland, 151 pp. The IPCC was established in 1988 by the *United Nations Environment Programme* and the *World Meteorological Organization* to offer scientific analysis on climate change and environmental damage.

The Ecotheological Shift in Biblical Interpretation

What has this environmental snapshot to do with biblical interpretation? I believe *everything*. Biblical interpreters invite a deep reflective spirit over the biblical text as they engage the world in which they live. Until recent decades, the traditional focus in biblical interpretation has been anthropocentric. This concerns the salvation of human beings, their relationship to God and Jesus and the act of God's liberation of humanity through the covenant and Jesus's enactment of the reign of God in word and deed.

Biblical interpreters, readers, and listeners can no longer engage the Bible without an awareness of the environmental context named above.[3] Our approach to engaging the Bible must offer a hermeneutic that considers creation and the wider network of living organisms. This requires a radical shift in ecological awareness and the emergence of an ecologically-oriented biblical hermeneutic. Such ecological consciousness can engage the biblical text and assist in the detection, naming, and expansion of anthropocentric exegetical approaches that have dominated biblical scholarship in recent decades. Given our environmental crisis and shifts in global ecological awareness, it is more pressing now for biblical interpreters to engage in an ecological hermeneutic. This calls for a movement from environmental *amnesia* to ecological *anamnesis* in the study of biblical texts. This world, the Earth, can inform the way we encounter the Bible. The ancient writers were not ecologists *per se*. In contrast to our contemporary penchant for digital preoccupation and individual lifestyles, however, the biblical writers would have been steeped in a cultural, social, and ecological environment that shaped the way they thought and reflected on God's and Jesus's encounter with the human and non-human world. They were sensitive to the way creation revealed the sacred.

Saint Bede (ca. 672–735 CE), for example, reflects on Luke 8:24, Jesus's calming a storm that threatens to annihilate the disciples in their boat. The calmness comes about, notes Bede, because of the response that creation offers to Jesus's action: every creature senses the Creator, because they are responsive to the majesty of the Creator. And what they sense is insensible to us.[4]

For Bede, creation (represented in the stormy sea) "senses" the presence of the Creator and responds to Jesus's action. This response, as Bede understands it, is because creation is more sensible or attuned than human beings to the presence of God. In this one gospel text, Bede exhibits an ecological or environmental *anamnesis* that helps him interpret a well-known nature miracle

---

[3] I prefer the expression of "listen to" the biblical text rather than "reading" it. Listening emphasises a dynamic of reception rather than control through reading which can be selective and determinative.

[4] Robert J. Karris, ed., *Works of St. Bonaventure: Commentary on the Gospel of Luke. Chapters 1–8* (Saint Bonaventure, NY: Franciscan Institute Publications, 2001), 693.

story from a different perspective. He honors and affirms the response of creation to the action of God.

Bede's interpretation represents an eighth century CE example of what might be identified in contemporary biblical exegesis as an ecological hermeneutic that complements a purely anthropocentric interpretation. Bede's focus here is not immediately on the rescue of the disciples but the response of the *natural world* to Jesus's action.

Approaches in Biblical Ecological Anamnesis

The Earth-Bible project represents one recent effort to be inclusive of the Earth in biblical interpretation.[5] Several ecological commentaries have already started to appear in this series. The principles of the project adopt an explicit ecological retrieval in interpreting the Bible. Further, the pioneering work of Vernon K. Robbins and the insights from the contributors to *Foundations for Sociorhetorical Explorations* offer further possibilities for engaging colleagues who are keen to move beyond the more formal-historical-literary biblical approaches to ones that are more socio-culturally sensitive. These allow room for an Earth listening, engagement, and hermeneutic. They present the possibility of moving from environmental *amnesia* to *anamnesia*. Elaine Wainwright, a contributor to the Earth-Bible project also acknowledges this. "We need," she writes, "a shift in the human social human imaginary … to examine much more intimately the complex interrelationships between and among all Earth-beings or Earth-constituents of all life-forms."[6]

Figures 3 to 5 (below) indicate the various possibilities that emerge. Figure 3 summarizes Robbins's approach in a familiar diagram that brings together the various texts and textures that open the biblical listener, reader, interpreter to the multiplicity of contexts that can shape the biblical text and its interpreter. Figure 4 is Wainwright's adjustment and addition to Robbins's contribution by adding an ecological texture to the biblical encounter. Figure 5 is my attempt to suggest that the whole interpretive praxis needs to be saturated with an ecological text. This text permeates everything: the author, readers/listeners, intertexts, texts, the Bible's Mediterranean context and the interpreter's world.

---

[5] Norman C. Habel and Peter Trudinger, eds., *Exploring Ecological Hermeneutics*, SymS 46 (Atlanta: Society of Biblical Literature, 2008).
[6] Elaine M. Wainwright, *Habitat, Human, and Holy: An Eco-rhetorical Reading of the Gospel of Matthew*, EBC 6 (Sheffield: Sheffield Phoenix, 2016), 25.

AN AUSTRALIAN ECOLOGICAL ENGAGEMENT 49

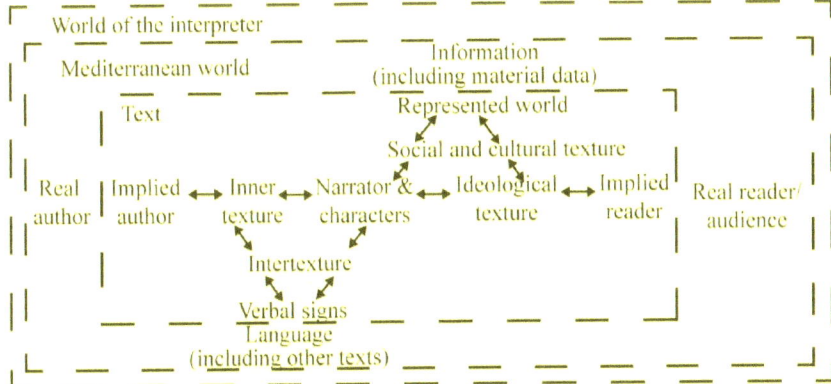

Fig. 3. Robbins's Sociorhetorical Exploration of a Biblical Text

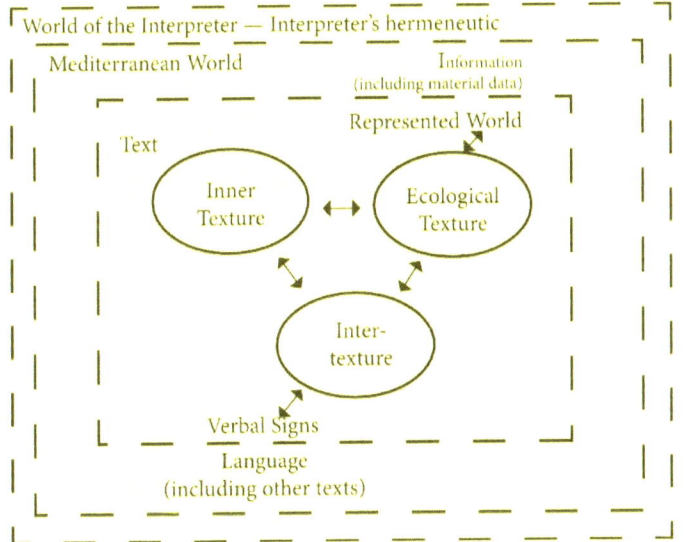

Fig. 4. Wainwright's adjustment to Robbins's Sociorhetorical Approach

Engaging *Foundations for Sociorhetorical Explorations*

The introduction to this volume summarizes the history, development, and present state of sociorhetorical interpretation (SRI), especially the textual strategies associated with inner texture, intertexture, social and cultural texture, ideological texture, and even sacred texture.[7] It also explicates how practitioners have expanded these strategies to include approaches that honor forms of discourse called "rhetorolects" and "rhetography." More pertinently, their practitioners encourage hermeneutical "expansion." They suggest that "SRI is identifiable by its energetic approach to multifaceted analysis of texts and its innovation when the hermeneutical analytic needs to be expanded."[8] This invitation for hermeneutical expansion provides the possibility for integrating an ecological hermeneutic into its methodology, especially in considering intertexture, inner texture, and the social and cultural dimensions of a biblical text.

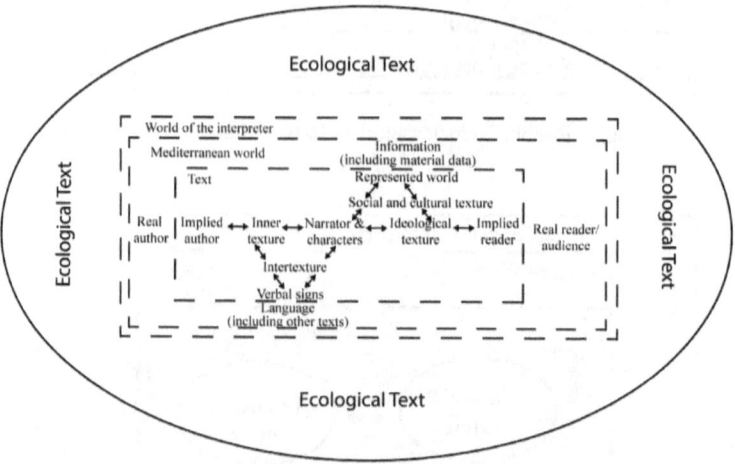

Fig. 5. The Ecological Climate ("Text") for Sociorhetorical Interpretation

- *Intertexture* concerns a text's reference to the world outside the text being interpreted (e.g., other texts, cultures, institutions, codes, relationships, places, etc.). Implicit in this is the ecological referent presumed by cultures, codes, relationships, and places. Our world is shaped by environmental networks and presuppositions, at times not explicated in the study of the physical and natural world in which a biblical text comes into being. This presumption, though, is what brings Wainwright to suggest a third texture, what she names "ecological texture."[9] Such an ecological anamnesis offers a further dimension for considering the environment that surrounds textual analytical engagement and its inner/outer texture.

---

[7] Vernon K. Robbins, Robert H. von Thaden Jr., and Bart B. Bruehler, eds., *Foundations for Sociorhetorical Exploration: A Rhetoric of Religious Antiquity Reader*, RRA 4 (Atlanta: SBL Press, 2016), 4.
[8] Robbins, *Foundations for Sociorhetorical Explorations*, 6.
[9] Wainwright, *Habitat, Human, and Holy*, 23.

- *Inner texture* concerns the textual-language patterns of communication by identifying a text's different textures (e.g., repetitive, progressive, narrational, opening-middle-closing, argumentative). However, in the present description, these textures focus on human patterns. They are anthropologically shaped. With an ecological anamnesis, the inner texture can also reveal a text's ecological or environmental resonances (what Wainwright calls "material and social actants").[10] This awareness offers a deeper richness unavailable in an anthropocentric textual focus.
- *Social and Culture texture* analyzes the social and culture context that locates a text within the social and culture world it evokes. This explicates a worldview that honors the living community that creates and formulates the text. This community lives within an environment and ecosystem that shapes it and the language that creates the biblical text. Further, the writing/reading community is also part of a network of organic and nonorganic matter, an ecological environment that influences the way biblical writers create their text.

Space prevents an ecological consideration of every essay in *Foundations for Sociorhetorical Explorations*. Common to all writers is the conviction that the biblical text is a social creation that reveals the social world or texture that shapes it. One texture that lends itself to investigation is *spatiality*. In what follows I intend to engage briefly three essays (in part 3 of *Foundations*) concerned with "Cultural Geography and Critical Spatiality." My intent is not to dismiss the fresh insights that emerge from the spatial enquiry their writers offer. Rather, I shall suggest that an analysis of a text's spatial inner texture might be expanded and enriched by an explicit ecological consciousness.

Spatiality as an Ecosystemic Reality

Jon L. Berquist begins the discussion with a helpful overview of theories of space and its constructed meaning in the ancient and biblical world.[11] He synthesizes the academic discourse about space that speaks of it as a given in any form of discourse—written or spoken.[12] He describes it in anthropocentric terms:

> Space has a genealogy and a history; it exists as a constructed category with the framework of human history. Space is something we make, create, produce, shape, reshape, form, inform, disform and transform.[13]

---

[10] Wainwright, *Habitat, Human, and Holy*, 23.
[11] Jon L. Berquist, "Theories of Space and Construction of the Ancient World," in Robbins, von Thaden, and Bruehler, *Foundations for Sociorhetorical Explorations*, 151–76.
[12] Berquist, "Theories of Space," 152.
[13] Berquist, "Theories of Space," 152.

From this perspective space is what human beings construct, shape, and act upon. It is a product of human endeavor and creativity. As Berquist moves to critical spatiality, he offers an aperture (or space!) for an ecotheological consideration. He recognizes that critical spatiality expands the discussion of spatiality beyond an essentialist frame of reference. "Critical spatiality," he suggests "understands all aspects of space to be human constructions that are socially contested."[14] This introduction of *social* contestation into the discussion could refer only to human engagement. But a consideration of socially contested space with an eco-systemic anamnesis also opens the possibility to consider space as deeply ecological, as part of the environment that is intimately located within human and public space, and features, perhaps unwittingly, in human interaction and encounter. Space is not only occupied and shaped by human beings. Ecosystems share and participate in space. To use Berquist's expression, space is "dynamically interrelated."[15] This links to the two essays which follow Berquist's exposé. Their writers engage spatial theory to "tell" the story of the temple[16] and as a framework for analyzing Luke 18:35–19:48.[17]

The Temple as an Ecological "Firstspace"

In her essay "Storied Space, or, Ben Sira 'Tells' a Temple," Claudia Camp draws on the works of several critical spatial theorists. She affirms, like Berquist, that critical spatiality is "not encountered as a transparent or objective 'reality' but is constructed in social practice."[18] Spatiality is a social reality which, I would add, has *ecological* implications.

Drawing on Henri Lefebvre's *Production of Space* (1991), Camp offers a triune interpretive paradigm of space:

- *Firstspace* (the "concrete materiality of spatial forms ... that can be empirically mapped");
- *Secondspace* (space imagined or thought about, in mental or cognitive form);
- *Thirdspace*: "lived realities as practiced" as people daily negotiate possible identities—it's the place of struggle and emancipation.[19] This last space is most helpful for biblical interpreters.

---

[14] Berquist, "Theories of Space," 154.
[15] Berquist, "Theories of Space," 169.
[16] Claudia V. Camp, "Storied Space, or, Ben Sira 'Tells' a 'Temple," in Robbins, von Thaden, and Bruehler, *Foundations for Sociorhetorical Explorations*, 177–96.
[17] Bart B. Bruehler, "From the Place: A Theoretical Framework for the Social-Spatial Analysis of Luke," *Foundations for Sociorhetorical Explorations*, 197–236.
[18] Camp, "Storied Space," 178.
[19] Camp, "Storied Space," 183.

Camp engages these three spaces and applies her spatial "trialectic" to the spatial discourse about the temple that saturates Sir 44–50. She interprets Ben Sira's temple as a negotiation between Third-, Second-, and Firstspaces. Her focus on Ben Sira's temple as a Thirdspace highlights it as "a monument to the male textual body," as "gynophobic" or misogynist.[20]

Toward the end of her essay, Camp suggests that Ben Sira's Thirdspace temple cannot be divorced from its Firstspace, the lived reality within a particular city composed of particular people. Ben Sira "lived in a real city … and worshiped in a real temple made of earthly substances."[21] This negotiation with Firstspace, as I understand Camp, offers the way of countering the hegemonic emphasis implied in Ben Sira's Thirdspace temple. Its environmental and ecological features were part of Firstspace which has ecological resonances. It is a real temple made of "earthly substances."

First Kings 5–8 describe well these substances: its walls and floors were constructed from cedar with ivory and gold inlay (1 Kgs 6:14–18); images of plants, palm trees and flowers decorated its walls (1 Kgs 6:18, 29); an olive-wood double door opened up to the Holy of Holies and the Ark of the Covenant, the symbolic navel of the universe; the temple's inner court had "three courses of dressed stone to one course of cedar beams" (1 Kgs 6:36);[22] on the sides of the temple's entrance were two great bronze pillars decorated with lily and pomegranate motifs (1 Kgs 7:15–22). From these pillars fire and smoke emerged, reminiscent of God's presence with the Israelites fleeing from Egypt (1 Kgs 7:15, 19, 21; 2 Chr 3:15); a large water-filled basin (called "the sea") decorated with various fruit themes inscribed into its bronze and supported by four groups of bronze bulls stood in one corner of the inner court (1 Kgs 7:23–26, 39, 44).

All of these images suggest that the temple's Firstspace was an ecosystemic map of the universe. Its ecological spatial contemplation could subvert the hegemonic emphasis uncovered in Camp's Thirdspace temple and revealed in Sirach. In other words, an explicit ecological focus can add a further dimension and critical contribution to a spatial enquiry of the temple.

Luke's Sycamore Tree (Luke 19:4) as Ecological Space

Something similar occurs when an ecological anamnesis is brought to a spatial study of a section of Luke's Gospel. It is here that I turn to Bart Bruehler's essay, "From This Place: A Theoretical Framework for the Social-Spatial Analysis of Luke." Bruehler critiques the dichotomization of the public and private sphere. He draws upon Robert David Sack's 1997 *Homo Geographicus* and uses his relational framework to illustrate how one's communal placement brings

---

[20] Camp, "Storied Space," 194, 195.
[21] Camp, "Storied Space," 194.
[22] NRSV.

with it different perspectives that influence culture and nature, a composite of social relations and shared meanings. I find Bruehler's study evocative. He reflects upon space and nature, dimensions I consider ecologically resonant: "The force of space," he writes, "is largely coterminous with nature. Space simply exists and is part of the natural world that human agents encounter (the focus of the natural sciences), and it acts as a force upon human existence. Nature affects us by means of the environment that surrounds, limits, and enables our lives."[23]

The symbiosis that Bruehler explicates here, that the natural world is part of space, is what human beings encounter. Bruehler quotes Sack a little later in his essay: "We humans are geographical beings transforming the earth and making it into a home, and that transformed world affects who we are."[24] The human species is *Homo Geographicus* avers Sack. It is also *Homo "Ecologicus."* We cannot ponder nature, space, and the identity of human beings only as "geographical beings" without an ecological awareness; we are indeed geographically oriented; we are also *ecological* beings, affected by the environment in which we live and upon which we act.

Sack's monodirectional anthropocentrism emphasizes human beings as the principal agents in our world. His approach could be extended to consider the transformational effect which Earth has on us. We are involved within an environmental network in a bidirectional process. We influence the world in which we live; it also deeply touches us; we are both environmental agents and ecological subjects.

This holistic appreciation coheres with Bruehler's critique of binary opposites detected in social-spatial exegesis and relational networks and is evident in the way that honor-shame and the public and private spheres are interpreted. Bruehler moves beyond the binary polarity of the public-private. He affirms the multivalency of space and demonstrates this in his study of Luke 18:35–19:48. He shows the slippage that occurs between the public and private spaces and how the public/private dichotomy disappears when one space is transformed by the other.[25] This occurs, for example, in the story of Zacchaeus's encounter with Jesus in Luke 19:1–10. Bruehler's spatial reconstruction focuses on domestic space. Jesus enters Zacchaeus's domestic space of private hospitality. Here, as the public and private become blurred, Jesus speaks to Zacchaeus's detractors, who seem also to be part of the space. One space (the public) invades the other (private); one space (the private) transforms the other (the public).

An ecological awareness to the story offers further insights which can enhance Bruehler's spatial enquiry. Zacchaeus's house is a private space where his encounter with Jesus becomes his conversion and transformation. It allows Jesus to address those who regard Zacchaeus as a sinner (Luke 19:7) and Luke's Gos-

---

[23] Bruehler, "From the Place," 199–200.
[24] Bruehler, "From the Place," 200.
[25] Bruehler, "From the Place," 229.

pel audience. The house is also an *ecological* space. Here, hospitality accompanied by Earth's gifts nurtures its guests—a theme familiar in other parts of the gospel. Besides Zacchaeus's house there is one other object ecologically prevalent in Luke's narrative.

Usually unnoticed by Lukan commentators is the story's environmental centerpiece, the sycamore tree. It is mentioned explicitly once (Luke 19:4) and implied in *three* moments in the encounter between Jesus and Zacchaeus: as Jesus first approaches Zacchaeus (Luke 19:5a); as he invites him "to come down" (Luke 19:5b),[26] and as Zacchaeus physically descends the tree (Luke 15:6). The tree, like Zacchaeus's house later, becomes an ecological space. It provides the setting for his experience of Jesus. Without its availability, the diminutive Zacchaeus would not be able to "see" Jesus, the verb twice mentioned by the evangelist (Luke 19:3–4) and the main purpose of Zacchaeus's hurried movement. Without its assistance Jesus would also not "see" Zacchaeus.

The tree, like the house, is a multivalent symbol: it provides a platform for Zacchaeus to "see" above the crowd. Its presence becomes the means for Zacchaeus finally to provide hospitality. The tree, like the house, also collapses the public-private dichotomy. While it exists in the public setting along with the crowd that surrounds it, the tree becomes a primary ecological symbol and the means of the private and personal encounter.

There are also other ecological themes that are part of Luke's story. These are evident in the theme of wealth associated with Zacchaeus, the confiscation of Earth's goods that has apparently contributed to Zacchaeus's social status, and his desire to bring about restitution for "things" that he might have accumulated in neglect of the poor. All of these confirm the ecological spatiality present within Luke's narrative and add another dimension to Bruehler's private-public spatial insights and enrich our interpretation of the story.

Conclusion

Foundations for Sociorhetorical Explorations offers biblical interpreters a fresh approach for engaging texts. Its writers remind us there are several ways that can allow us to see the meaning of biblical texts no longer determined by one approach that has held hegemony over exegetical interpretation. This is the historical-form-critical exegetical method that has dominated biblical interpretation. SRI is an approach that honors the textual dynamic, all those texts that highlight the cultural and social environment that shapes a text.

I have suggested in this essay that SRI can naturally incorporate an ecological anamnesis to remind us that the biblical text is also an ecological intertext. This has hermeneutical implications as we seek to engage the critical environ-

---

[26] NRSV.

mental realities that globally confront us and allow us to be more sensitive to the physical environment in which we live.

To return to where I began, this is a critical time in our history. Earth consciousness is not an option; biblical interpreters can assist readers/listeners to the biblical stories to critique a pervasive and dominant anthropocentric exclusivism forgetful of the environment in which we live. The voice of Pope Francis is helpful here. He criticizes an anthropocentricism that is oblivious to the environment and views the natural world merely as a place for refuse:

> Modern anthropocentrism has paradoxically ended up prizing technical thought over reality, since "the technological mind sees nature as an insensate order, as a cold body of facts, as a mere 'given', as an object of utility, as raw material to be hammered into useful shape; it views the cosmos similarly as a mere 'space' into which objects can be thrown with complete indifference...."[27]

A retrieval of ecological anamnesis for biblical interpretation, coherent with and implicit in SRI, can assist biblical readers/listeners in deepening their spirit of ecological ascetism and environmental care. It might even help to rescue, besides other parts of our world where there is environmental damage, the Great Barrier Reef.

---

[27] Pope Francis, *Laudato Si: On Care for our Common Home* (Vatican City: Vatican Press, 2015), paragraph 115, quoting Pope John Paul II's Encyclical Letter *Centesimus Annus* (Vatican City: Vatican Press, 1991), 38.

Enacting Sociorhetorical Interpretation in the Island Nation of Samoa in Oceania

Vaitusi Nofoaiga

Introduction

It is a privilege to be given the opportunity by Vernon K. Robbins to respond to the multiauthor volume: *Foundations for Sociorhetorical Exploration: A Rhetoric of Religious Antiquity Reader*. I was asked to make a response on the essays that are most helpful and/or interesting in the volume for the way I approach and use sociorhetorical interpretation (SRI); whether there are gaps in the volume for me; and what additional considerations could or should have been in the volume to help and encourage approaches like mine. My response is based on these important questions that are discussed in the following sections. I begin with a description of my approach and use of SRI, followed by discussion of that approach utilizing the essays chosen from the volume. The final section is a conclusion that offers a few recommendations on what could be added in the next stage of the development of SRI, which would help and encourage approaches like mine that considers important the experience of the reader in today's world.

My Understanding and Use of Robbins's Sociorhetorical Approach

As a reader of the Bible from our island nation of Samoa in Oceania, I have been trying to find ways of approaching and reading the Bible that would help make better sense of Jesus's proclamation of God's kingdom in the reality of the contemporary Samoan world. This endeavor is prompted by my experience and understanding that some social, cultural, and economic problems occurring in families in the Samoan community are outcomes of our people's utter commitment to fulfilling traditional interpretations of the Bible brought into Samoa by the early missionaries. One example of these traditional interpretations is the belief in a discipleship that promotes the idea that caring for church needs is more important than caring for family needs. This belief has been asserted by traditional interpretations of Jesus's calling fishermen to follow him (Matt 4:18–25),[1] and Jesus's refusal to let one of his disciples go bury his father (Matt 8:21–22).[2] These interpretations show Jesus's attitude toward the family in the local context as a secondary priority. The problem that arises from these so-called traditional interpretations is that attention has tended to focus on the global function and significance of Jesus's ministry.[3] I have witnessed and heard of family struggles and blaming of the gospel in our Samoan society as a result of practicing these traditional interpretations. The point is that some of these traditional interpretations contradict the egalitarian love of God proclaimed in the Bible—the unconditional love of God for all spaces, places, times, and people.

In other words, some aspects of traditional interpretations of the Bible no longer reflect the reality of life encountered by some Christians in the twenty-first century, such as our Christian nation of Samoa. For me, upholding these traditional interpretations as being the only true and relevant ones is a direct result of the conservative consideration of these so-called traditional methods of reading the Bible as the only acceptable methods of reading in biblical criticism. For example, historical and literary criticisms have become established as dominant approaches to biblical interpretation. Thus, upholding the traditional methods of reading as the authoritative critical approaches to interpreting the Bible determines the most authentic interpretation. As Fernando F. Segovia observes:

> since for historical criticism the text as means possessed a univocal and objective meaning and since this could be retrieved via a properly informed and conducted scientific inquiry, the meaning uncovered was for all times and cultures…. In other words, the original meaning of the text, properly secured and

---

[1] See Stephen Barton, *Discipleship and Family Ties in Mark and Matthew*, SNTSMS 80 (Cambridge: Cambridge University Press, 1994), 23–56. Jack D. Kingsbury, *Matthew as Story*, 2nd ed. (Philadelphia: Fortress, 1988), 40, 130–31.

[2] See Gerd Theissen, *The First Followers of Jesus: A Sociological Analysis of the Earliest Christianity*, trans. John Bowden (London: SCM, 1978), 10–14; Jack D. Kingsbury, "On Following Jesus: The 'Eager' Scribe and the 'Reluctant' Disciple (Matthew 18:18–22)," *NTS* 34 (1998): 45–59.

[3] As Halvor Moxnes suggests: "his (Jesus) origin in terms of place and household has not evoked much interest. The question of his family is mostly relegated to a less important biographical interest. In a similar manner his critical elements about family and household, and about leaving family, become just a topic, and not a very important one, in the overall picture of Jesus' message. This seems to be typical of recent Christian scholarship on Jesus." Halvor Moxnes, *Putting Jesus in His Place: A Radical Vision of Household and Kingdom* (Louisville: Westminster John Knox, 2003), 23.

established, could dictate and govern the overall boundaries or parameters of the Christian life everywhere and at all times.[4]

I do not nullify the traditional methods and traditional interpretations these methods produced. In fact, I consider them very important. However, it is also important to consider other approaches and interpretations such as those that signify readers' location and situation in today's world.[5] Considering readers' situation to be important in biblical criticism, which emerged in the mid-1970s, brought another dimension into reading the Bible.[6] This is reflected in my understanding of Gadamer's aesthetic theory, which provides a backdrop to how I approach the Bible using sociorhetorical interpretation in my worlds—such as my social and cultural Samoan world and my world as an academician.[7]

In this theory, Gadamer compares the question of meaning to the experience of art. The main question for Gadamer is how we can find the meaning of art or true beauty of art. Gadamer contends that artwork has the artist's world behind it, for the artist produced the artwork. The art is left by itself and it has its own world. When it is experienced aesthetically by a viewer, it is viewed from the world of the spectator. This experiencing of art is called "play." The spectator has brought to the artwork his or her pre-understanding of the art. At the meeting point, the art is transformed into reality at the moment of viewing. Gadamer talks about play as a contemporary movement that brings out the meaning of the art. In connection with the literary text, Gadamer suggests that, like the experience of works of art, reading takes place at the moment when the "play movement" occurs. Thus, the task of a reader is to break from the influence of classical hermeneutics that restricts interpretation to one direction. Encountering a work of art or a text, we experience it in relation to our situations and locations.

---

[4] Fernando F. Segovia, *Decolonizing Biblical Studies: A View from the Margins* (New York: Orbis, 2000), 14.
[5] Feminist Criticism, as the most prominent among those approaches, is a well-known form of biblical criticism which engages the text and challenges dominant methods of interpretation through the filters of social and political concerns, and the interests of women. See Elaine M. Wainwright, "Feminist Criticism and the Gospel of Matthew," in *Methods for Matthew*, ed. Mark Allan Powell (Cambridge: Cambridge University Press, 2009), 83–117. Other approaches include Postcolonial Criticism and Islander Criticism.
[6] See Fernando F. Segovia, "And They Began to Speak in Other Tongues: Competing Modes of Discourse in Contemporary Biblical Criticism," in *Reading from This Place: Social Location and Biblical Interpretation in the United States*, ed. Fernando Segovia and Mary Ann Tolbert, vol. 1 (Minneapolis: Fortress, 1995), 1–34; R. S. Sugirtharajah, ed., *Vernacular Hermeneutics* (Cambridge: Cambridge University Press, 2009).
[7] Hans-Georg Gadamer, *Truth and Method*, trans. Joel Weinsheimer and Donald G Marshall (New York: Seabury, 1975), 91–102; 112–16; 147; 273–81; 356–57.

The shift from the classical emphasis to the consideration of readers' locations has raised questions regarding how the practitioners and proponents of the traditional methods of biblical criticism understood the reader.[8] These practitioners and proponents of the traditional methods come from a wide range of social and geographical locations; yet, they overlook the perspectives and agendas of readers whose understanding of the text are necessarily affected by their own social, cultural, economic, religious, and political locations and situations. I have found in Robbins's sociorhetorical approach the significance of considering how readers' situations and locations are vital in the process of interpretation. This is one of the reasons why I admire sociorhetorical interpretation as reflected in the following explanation of my understanding of Robbins's sociorhetorical approach.

Vernon K. Robbins developed sociorhetorical interpretation as the integration of a social science approach with literary-based advances in biblical studies.[9] His goal was to develop a rhetorical approach that combined literary, social, cultural, and ideological issues in the interpretation of biblical texts. Sociorhetorical interpretation recognizes that a world is encoded in the text in and through its language.[10] Sociorhetorical criticism provides tools for interpreters to examine how the text's language shapes meanings and allows readers to relate those meanings to their own world in order to make meaning relevant.[11] Readers with different insights from diverse locations may interpret the same text with differing meanings.[12] In this way, sociorhetorical interpretation is not meant to nullify other methods and interpretations but to enter into dialogue with them, so that new meanings are produced and made relevant to other worlds and locations. This part of the sociorhetorical approach is important in two ways. First, it allows my Samoan world to be part of the interpretation and analysis of the text. Second, it affirms that my interpretation does not need to nullify traditional

---

[8] The historical outline of the progress of hermeneutics is briefly explained in David Jasper, *A Short Introduction to Hermeneutics* (Louisville: Westminster John Knox, 2004).

[9] Vernon K. Robbins, *Exploring the Texture of Texts: A Guide to Socio-rhetorical Interpretation* (Harrisburg: Trinity Press International, 1996), 1.

[10] Robbins, *Exploring the Texture of Texts*, 1–2. See also Elaine M. Wainwright's explanation of this combination in her article, "Reading Matthew 3–4: Jesus—Sage, Seer, Sophia, Son of God," *JSNT* 77 (2000): 28–29.

[11] Robbins, *Exploring the Texture of Texts*, 1.

[12] Vernon K. Robbins, *The Invention of Christian Discourse*, vol. 1 (Dorset UK: Deo, 2009), 5: "A socio-rhetorical interpretive analytic applies a politics of invitation, with a presupposition that the people invited into the conversation will contribute significantly new insights as a result of their particular experiences, identities, and concerns. In other words, a socio-rhetorical interpretive analytic presupposes genuine teamwork: people from different locations and identities working together with different cognitive frames for the purpose of getting as much insight as possible on the relation of things to one another."

interpretations. It is not meant to impose the reader's location and situation on the text but to interact with the text, seeking how the text can answer one's questions. In this way, detailed attention is given to the text itself.

Two questions determine how I bring myself using SRI into the interpretive process. First, how does the sociorhetorical approach allow my world, represented by a hermeneutic from my world as Samoan, to become part of the interpretive process? Second, when my world as a reader enters the process, how does the sociorhetorical approach deal with my interaction with the text?

The answer to the first question lies in what *sociorhetorical* means. Robbins explains that *socio* indicates the anthropological and sociological factors and characteristics of sociorhetorical interpretation such as "social class, social systems, personal and community status, people on the margins, and people in position of power."[13] And *rhetorical* defines how the language in a text is used as a tool of communication.[14] Simply put, the sociorhetorical approach explores how language reflects and communicates the influences of social and cultural values and beliefs on the lives of people (no matter what their faith commitments are). It is these values and beliefs that I analyze using hermeneutics from my Samoan world such as the hermeneutic of *tautuaileva* (serve in-between spaces) and the hermeneutic of *fiaola* (opportunity seeker) that I used to read discipleship and Jesus's ministry in the Gospel of Matthew.[15]

The answer to my second question is made evident in Robbins's diagram of the "socio-rhetorical model of textual communication."[16] In the interaction between the reader and the text, the outside rectangle represents the world of the readers. This world is the location for the interaction of readers' personal lives and times with "the historical, social, cultural, ideological and religious worlds (encoded in the text)."[17] It is a world constructed of diverse ideologies. There are boundaries that divide the worlds of the interpreter, the text, and the author, but these boundaries are represented by broken lines that allow the interactions between those worlds, letting the meaning of the text and the effects of that meaning travel between them.[18]

---

[13] Robbins, *Exploring the Texture of Texts*, 1.
[14] Robbins, *Exploring the Texture of Texts*, 1.
[15] See Vaitusi Nofoaiga, *A Samoan Reading of Discipleship in Matthew*, IVBS 8 (Atlanta: SBL Press, 2017).
[16] See Vernon K. Robbins, *The Tapestry of Early Christian Discourse: Rhetoric, Society and Ideology* (New York: Routledge, 1996), 21.
[17] Robbins, *Tapestry of Early Christian Discourse*, 24.
[18] Robbins, *Tapestry of Early Christian Discourse*, 22.

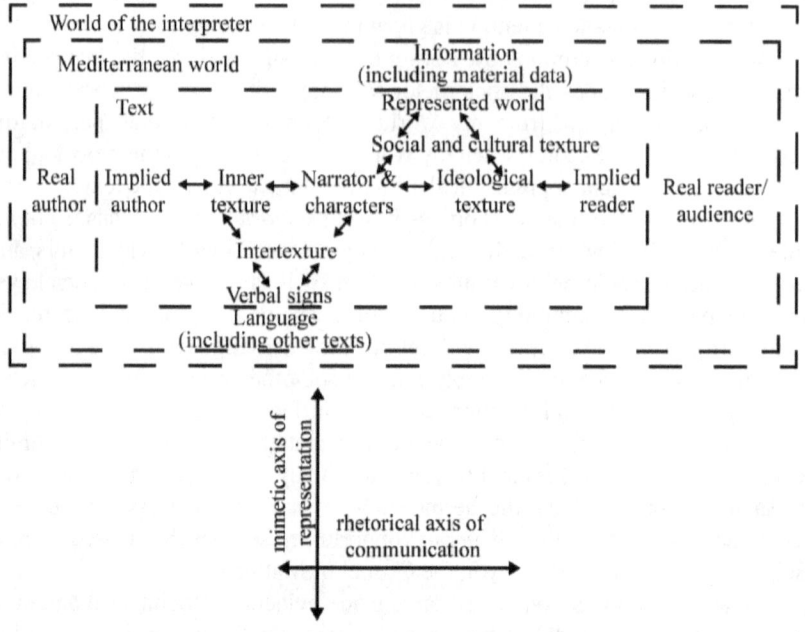

Fig. 1. Robbins's Sociorhetorical Model of Textual Interpretation

From exploring the subject of discipleship in the gospels, I see that these broken lines allow interaction between my Samoan world about serving the needs of local family members in *fa'a Samoa* (Samoan social and cultural ways) and the Christian teachings about discipleship to travel to and from the world encoded in the gospel texts. In this way, sociorhetorical interpretation facilitates how I in the Samoan world, with the tensions in its egalitarian and marginalizing cultures, might read the world encoded in the gospel texts such as Matthew. More importantly, it provides a way to explore marginality in the world of the gospel authors as it is encoded in the text. Therefore, sociorhetorical interpretation offers a framework that facilitates consideration of the needs of local family members in the biblical text. This brings my Samoan world into dialogue with the selected texts toward producing other interpretations alongside traditional interpretations.[19] There is temptation in bringing readers' locations or situations into the process of interpretation to impose their own contexts on interpretation of the text. Regarding temptations to contextualize and appropriate, my use of SRI with a hermeneutics from my world as a reader of the Bible does not deliver the usual contextual reading whereby something from my culture is appropriated

---

[19] Robbins, *Tapestry of Early Christian Discourse*, 11.

to make sense of, and thereby authorize (for my social and cultural world), biblical texts. Rather, my reading approach negotiates the rhetorical world encoded in the text with the sociohistorical world of the first century CE in a way that allows other Samoan readers to read between rigid historicism and formal literarism. In this way of approaching the text from my situation as a reader of the Bible in my Samoan context, the focus of the whole process of interpretation is the text. Thus, the function of my reader's situation in the process is not to impose my situation or context on the text, but only to raise questions that guide the exploration of the selected texts. In this way, signifying my location as a reader provides the lenses to see and approach the text, thereby exploring the text with my Samoan lenses in order to take advantage of the multifaceted and interdisciplinary function of sociorhetorical interpretation as the interpretive tool. This is my approach or use of SRI that is the basis for the next part of my response, which is my reflection on certain essays from the volume.

My Response to Essays

The first essay by Robbins[20] is one I find most helpful and interesting as it indicates glimpses of my approach and use of SRI. The essay begins with description of the emergence of sociorhetorical interpretation, the characteristics or elements of which are what attracted my attention as a reader of the Bible in the first place. Robbins's description of these elements reflects my approach that I described above and will now talk about.

First, according to Robbins, the development of SRI in the beginning makes known the interdisciplinary, multifaceted, and self-conscious practices of interpretation and reflection that have become the significant characteristics of SRI. Robbins mentions the challenges encountered by scholars of the New Testament, which produced an atmosphere where rhetorical analysis in conjunction with the social sciences and ideological criticism brought about the reworking of boundaries and new approaches in the interpretation of biblical and related literature in the 1990s. The first challenge put forward by Amos Wilder was to encourage scholars to reconsider the rhetoric of biblical texts as religious and aesthetic discourse. The next challenge by Wayne Meeks and Jonathan Z. Smith was to use anthropological and sociological tools in the interpretation of early Christianity and its socially embedded and encoded texts. During this time, Wilhelm Wuellner and Elisabeth Schüssler Fiorenza emphasized consideration of the political and ideological nature of biblical texts. Robbins was able to put all these chal-

---

[20] Vernon K. Robbins, "Sociorhetorical Criticism: Mary, Elizabeth, and the Magnificat as a Test Case," in *Foundations for Sociorhetorical Exploration: A Rhetoric of Religious Antiquity Reader*, ed. Vernon K. Robbins, Robert H. von Thaden Jr., and Bart B. Bruehler, RRA 4 (Atlanta: SBL Press, 2016), 29–74.

lenges and their influences in the beginning process of establishing the four textures of SRI.

Second, the development of SRI and the challenges faced by practitioners of New Testament interpretation that resulted in the four textures of SRI brings about the following characteristic of SRI that I find very important as a reader of the Bible from Oceania. SRI considers the self-conscious practices of interpretation and reflection to be of primary importance in its programmatic, multi-strategic approach. The self-conscious approach is part of my use of SRI. It is where I insert my self-consciousness as a reader into the process of the interpretation of the text. This is carried out by considering the text as having a world of its own or having its own beauty. My earlier description of Gadamer's "aesthetic" theory reflects this consideration. As described by Robbins, this characteristic is encouraged by Amos Wilder in the reconsideration of the rhetoric of biblical texts as religious and aesthetic discourse. It is part of the reworking and the shifting of boundaries of rhetorical analysis which opens up interesting and exciting dialogue with other disciplines such as spatiality and the cognitive sciences. This essay by Robbins is very important, for it demonstrates how SRI works, reworks, and shifts the boundaries of rhetorical analysis.

Robbins's interpretation of the *Magnificat* in Luke's Gospel in this essay is a prime example. The part of his interpretation that I wish to emphasize is Robbins's consideration of ideology to recognize that every text has an implicit politics. For Robbins, Mary is obviously looked at as an unmarried, pregnant, and dishonored woman in the story. However, her character as a woman chosen to bear Jesus the Son of God presents a winning approach and action for the early Christians. Despite the impact of patriarchal and patronage structures that existed in the time of the story, Mary as a person chosen by God, was able to encourage peace and harmony. Also important, as shown in Robbins's emphasis on openness to new boundaries and ideology, he evokes another interpretation of Mary's relationship to Elizabeth. Their relationship as women in the story destroys rivalries among women and wives over their children. Instead, they present a community living in peace. I can relate to this use of an ideology from the point of view of a reader in today's world, such as a reader from my island context. The story of Mary's relationship with Elizabeth can be viewed as a story of *nofotane* (women living with their husbands with their husbands' families or village).

Other essays that I have found very significant and interesting are those addressing the function of topoi. I will respond briefly to two essays with this concern by George A. Kennedy and Carolyn R. Miller. First, Kennedy's essay which speaks of the visual aspects of Greek topoi.[21] According to Kennedy, Aristotle's view of perception and image is inherent in language. It is Aristotle's

---

[21] George A. Kennedy, "Reworking Aristotle's Rhetoric," in Robbins, von Thaden, and Bruehler, *Foundations for Sociorhetorical Exploration*, 77–93.

emphasis on "seeing or observing" that evokes a sense of the existence of phenomena in physical space and these are very common motifs in his work. These phenomena are topoi (places) where topics are to be found that influence persuasive reasoning. As an island reader of the Bible, seeing and observing are very important life skills. For example, seeing and observing the best time and weather for fishing in a particular ocean or when to plant and harvest a particular crop is a task of discovery that leads us to the task of inventing the best tools or equipment for carrying out those tasks. It is one of our ways of reading our physical, ecological, and geographical topoi which we keep in our oral traditions passed from one generation to another, through our traditional songs, dances, and cultural practices. It is where we create and invent our rhetoric of Samoan social and cultural speeches that are spoken and shared mainly by our paramount chiefs (*matai*) when families and villages gather for special occasions. This is also reflected in Robbins's emphasis on rhetography, which I will talk about later. Robbins's sociorhetorical approach allows us—other readers of the Bible—to use our own worlds or topoi as departure points for approaching the Bible.

In my use of SRI, my entrance to the text is guided by my own experience and understanding of my world. Part of it is my understanding of place in my Samoan social and cultural world. According to Charles Taylor, "we cannot understand another society until we have understood ourselves better as well."[22] In other words, my understanding of topoi in rhetoric embedded in the text comes from understanding of place as a physical and geographical place. Part of my response to Kennedy's and Miller's essays is to explain my understanding of place in my location as a reader of the Bible, and how it leads to my exploration of the topoi in the text using SRI.

I consider *place* important in identifying my location as a reader and this consideration helps guide my approaching the text using SRI. To identify myself in relation to place is defining what identity is. According to the *Oxford English Dictionary*, identity means "the quality or condition of being the same substance, composition, nature, properties, or in particular qualities under consideration; absolute or essential sameness; oneness."[23] This speaks of identity as defining how I am the same as and distinct from others—in other words, who I can be identified with either in accordance with my individual characteristics or in regard to the characteristics of a group of people to which I belong. Generally, according to this definition, there are different types of identities. However, identifying who I am focuses mainly on my social and cultural identity as Samoan in relation to my understanding of Samoa as a local place, one with its own culture, values, spaces, and people. This focus is based on my un-

---

[22] Charles Taylor, *Philosophy and the Human Sciences: Philosophical Papers* (Cambridge: Cambridge University Press, 1985), 129.
[23] *OED* online, s.v. "Identity."

derstanding of the Samoan social and cultural world as the lens that informs my seeing, experiencing, and exploring of everyday life. Therefore, to introduce what identity means to me as a Samoan I use the character of being a servant in Samoan culture, as expressed and pictured in its culture of service. This culture of service describes a Samoan who knows his or her role as a member of a Samoan family and village, that is, one who is able to listen, see, and feel the needs of family and village, and act in fulfillment of them, despite the challenges encountered in doing so. Indeed, identity is not just about identifying persons according to the culture to which they belong, but also about how they put that culture into action. Thus, identity is action-in-progress that is persistently shaped by the changes people encounter in the world/s in which they live. In this way, my sense of identity is not static but dynamic.

But that sense of identity cannot be felt and understood without a sense of place. The *Oxford Dictionary of Geography* defines place as "a particular point on earth's surface; an identifiable location for a situation imbued with human values."[24] What this means is that place is a certain point on earth identified by how a group of people live in that place in terms of their values. This implies that place is not just a location. It is also a space that is identified by the various situations emergent from interactions among people in terms of their human values. Thus, place is a location and a space lived in and controlled by people. It is the environment where I learn how to live and relate to other people. It is also the environment where I experience familiar and unfamiliar situations based on the human values accepted by people who inhabit that place. In this way, understanding the particular place where I belong in a society determines how I see and experience other places. More importantly, it shapes how I see other people in other places. Thus, a sense of place is important in defining who I am as a Samoan.

My sense of belonging as shown here leads me to the text, exploring what is place or topos in the text and people who belong to those places. In our Samoan social and cultural world, we have in our oral traditions a "special rhetoric of place" where certain place names are connected to particular gods, waters, trees, houses, rocks, fine mats, and title names (*matai*—paramount chiefs*)* are embedded. This is what needs to be explored more from my own world as a Samoan reader in the use of SRI. How can SRI bring in our different and diverse rhetorics in our oral traditions into reading biblical texts without imposing them on those texts?

This point is reflected in Carolyn R. Miller's essay.[25] Miller's essay speaks of the Aristotelian topoi as resources for rhetorical invention. The purpose of this

---

[24] Susan Mayhew, *A Dictionary of Geography* (Oxford: Oxford University Press, 1997), 327.

[25] Carolyn R. Miller, "The Aristotelian Topos: Hunting for Novelty," in Robbins, von Thaden, and Bruehler, *Foundations for Sociorhetorical Exploration*, 95–117.

essay is to find how the Aristotelian concept of topos contributes to the current interest in generative rhetoric. Aristotle makes topoi function rhetorically as conceptual places to which an arguer goes mentally to find arguments. For Miller, the powerful intuition of Aristotle can be elaborated and articulated into a neo-Aristotelian theory of invention.

In doing so, Miller discusses the difference between invention and discovery in rhetoric. According to Miller, invention has a twofold meaning. One is about arranging something to happen that never existed, and the other is about coming upon what already exists or is discovered. These definitions relate to modernism and postmodernism. Discovery as invention is the emphasis of modernism, where understanding topoi is determined by set objectives. Invention as "coming to be" is the emphasis of postmodernism. For Miller, how can this understanding articulate a new Aristotelian theory of invention? Miller suggests considering topos as a spatial metaphor that takes the meaning and use of topos to a level beyond topos itself. Attribution of one's knowledge into defining and creating a topos brings another dimension into finding a meaning for topos. Miller brings space into topos where searching past experiences, examining new circumstances, and finding other options is carried out, producing new possible meanings and interpretations. This part of Miller's essay that emphasizes hunting for novelty of something new and unusual reflects how I use SRI from my locations as a reader of the Bible described above. But how can topoi as resources for rhetorical invention in oral tradition be used to discover meanings of topoi in a text? Kennedy's emphasis on the visual aspects of Greek topoi is one way of doing my approach, which is to begin with what I view from my location as a reader.

Robbins's essay, "Rhetography: A New Way of Seeing the Familiar Text," speaks of the significance of visual aspects of texts where readers and hearers create graphic images in their minds.[26] It is communicating a context of meaning to hearers and readers. Robbins argues that interpretation influenced by classical rhetoric has emphasized speech (logos) in texts. From the sociorhetorical perspective, this approach has given attention to rhetology, namely reasoning and argumentation, without recognizing the significant part played by rhetography in the interpretation. In other words, there has been a rhetorical focus on the rhetology of texts, which is the natural heritage from classical rhetorical interpretation, rather than a focus on the blending of reasoning and picturing in rhetology. The problem that arises from emphasizing the tradition of classical rhetoric is the placing of the rhetography of the judicial, deliberative, and epideictic rhetoric in the background, namely, reducing the speaker (ethos) and audience (pathos) as a context of communicating meaning to a location behind

---

[26] Vernon K. Robbins, "Rhetography: A New Way of Seeing the Familiar Text," in Robbins, von Thaden, and Bruehler, *Foundations for Sociorhetorical Exploration*, 329–64.

the scene. Depending on the logos or speech in the text does not suffice to reveal the meaning or generative meanings of the text—meanings prompted by various and different picturing in the text. The problem of focusing attention completely on the rhetology of a text is that it ignores other interpretations and meanings that could be produced by picturing other types of speakers and audiences in the mind. Because of this problem, Robbins turns to George Kennedy's work that observes a blending of what Kennedy called "worldly" rhetoric in New Testament texts, which Robbins considers the focus on rhetology of New Testament texts, and what Kennedy called "radical" rhetoric.

According to Robbins, radical rhetoric is the rhetography of New Testament discourse that presupposes contexts in God's created and uncreated world, rather than contexts in the classical city-state. Robbins's goal is to show that Kennedy's work should not be taken as a final statement about the nature of New Testament rhetoric in relation to classical rhetoric, but as an investigation that exhibits blending of worldly and radical rhetoric that New Testament rhetorical interpreters need to analyze and interpret carefully. In other words, the issue raised focuses on how the picturing of the speaker and audience can help the interpretations of the logos (speech). However, my question is: what about the reader now, especially the Island reader? From my experience of life, I picture things that are both helpful and not. Picturing from my point of view as a Samoan is dealing with how to survive. It is rhetography from my own world that leads me to viewing the logos in relation to the speakers and audience of that logos. This is the challenge for me, that is, how my picturing of life in my own world as an Island reader of the text informs my picturing of the text.

In this regard, Robert H. Von Thaden's essay provides an answer.[27] Von Thaden emphasizes the significance of what he called "a cognitive turn" which is a conceptual blending within the sociorhetorical framework. Cognition is acquiring understanding through experience and observation unlike reasoning that is based on hard evidences. Conceptual Integration theory emphasizes how language propels and prompts meaning and when combined with SRI it becomes a very effective interpretive tool. It is where readers' knowledge and experience is brought into the interaction between the reader and the text. Focusing only on the logos embedded in the text to determine the true meaning of the text is the weakness of historical critics. But von Thaden's suggestion of considering cognition as part of approaching the text offers biblical scholars like us in Oceania, a world far away from Jerusalem where the story of Jesus emerged, other ways of making sense of the meaning of the Bible in our own world. In other words, considering the knowledge and experience from our worlds as being important in the interpretation of the text will make us think again about going all the way

---

[27] Robert H. von Thaden Jr., "A Cognitive Turn: Conceptual Blending within a Sociorhetorical Framework," in Robbins, von Thaden, and Bruehler, *Foundations for Sociorhetorical Exploration*, 285–328.

to Jerusalem to look for evidences to prove whether there was a person named Jesus walking on earth in the first century! Our attention as readers, therefore, should be about finding how the story of Jesus, now embedded in the logos and pictures of the language of the Bible, makes sense in how we live life as Christians in our worlds.

Conclusion

This volume offers very important information on SRI that we as readers of the Bible from Oceania should use to make relevant the meaning and message of the gospels in our worlds. I have mentioned above some important points, which can be understood through the emphasis I place on the part of Robbins's diagram of the "socio-rhetorical model of textual communication" that shows how we can use our knowledge and experience of our worlds in the interpretation of the text. This also coincides with the main aspect that I would like the next volume of SRI to focus upon—showing how readers' situations and locations in today's world could be used with SRI to approach and read the text. This is where we bring into the reading and interpretation of the Bible our own rhetoric of discovery and invention from our world's oral traditions and orality to explore the rhetoric of discovery and invention embedded in the language of the text of the Bible. This is important because in my understanding and use of SRI as shown in this volume, it offers the significance of the negotiating of values and relations between the reader and the text. Thus, interpretation invites the engaging of the workings of orality not only behind the text, but also the orality in front of the text as a rhetorical device, that will make the significance of the gospel more meaningful in our worlds. With these points in mind, SRI will continue to be an interesting, exciting, and relevant interpretive analytic for us in our unique worlds.

Fāiā Analysis of Romans 13:1–7: Integrating a Samoan Perspective with Sociorhetorical Interpretation

Fatilua Fatilua

Reading Rom 13:1–7 within the nexus of church and state is especially worrisome in today's political environment.[1] While there are other contexts to consider, my interest lies in recent developments in Samoa, in particular the marginalization of religious institutions. First, the sitting government in 2017 amended the constitution declaring Samoa a nation founded on the Triune God.[2] Prior to the amendment, language stipulating the extent to which Christian principles apply in Samoan society appeared only in the preamble. Not only does the new law alienate all non-Christian religions in the country, it effectively weakens religious freedom and nondiscrimination in Samoa, indispensable pillars in any modern democracy.[3]

---

[1] I am mindful of the recent case in which Attorney General Jeff Sessions of the United States government cited Rom 13 in support of the Administration's policy regarding the treatment of undocumented aliens at the Mexican Border: Lincoln Mullen, "The Fight to Define Romans 13," *The Atlantic*, 15 June 2018, https://tinyurl.com/SBL3814b. I am also cognizant of the ongoing struggle in countries like Zambia as a result of the nexus between church and state: Isabel Apawo Phiri, "President Frederick J. T. Chiluba of Zambia: The Christian Nation and Democracy," *Journal of Religion in Africa* 33 (2003): 401–28. See also Jonathan A. Draper, "'Humble Submission to Almighty God' and Its Biblical Foundation: Contextual Exegesis of Romans 13:1–7," *Journal of Theology for Southern Africa* 63 (1988): 30–38 for the South African apartheid government's use of Rom 13.
[2] Grant Wyeth, "Samoa Officially Becomes a Christian State: The Constitutional Change Is Aimed at Avoiding Religious Unrest," *The Diplomat*, 16 June 2017.
[3] Bal Kama, "Christianising Samoa's Constitution and Religious Freedom in the Pacific" DevPolicy Blog, 27 April 2017, https://tinyurl.com/SBL3814c.

Second, the marginalization of religious institutions is further evident in the dispute regarding the new law to tax all church ministers.[4] While it strengthens government revenue, the new law undermines longstanding tradition concerning religion in Samoan society. The government, in efforts to appease public outcry, dangles Rom 13 as basis for compliance. That the Samoan government holds a particular interpretation of Paul's injunction to submit to governing authorities is a cause for concern, and the reason for this paper. Drawing on Pacific indigenous knowledge, integrated with aspects of sociorhetorical interpretation, the aim is to render an alternative reading of Paul, and to challenge a cultural framework that has long guided the church in Samoa.[5]

Much can be learned from using a Samoan reading to reorient the passage, to make it more meaningful within the Samoan context and the Pacific context.[6] For this purpose, I use the Samoan formative phrase *fāiā-i-upu-ma-fatua'iupu* (relation in words and word constructions).[7]

Fāiā: Emphasizing Relations and Connections in the Text

The word *fāiā* (bridge), conveys a sense of connection or relation.[8] One can envision, for example, putting a log to cross from one side of a river bank to the other. The log represents the *fāiā*, the bridge, the connection. But it is more than just a connection. *Fāiā* recognizes space in between, acknowledging gaps and voids. It explores ways to make connections among things otherwise isolated and separated.

A word of caution is offered here. *Fāiā* can be burdensome and problematic. A disconnection often emerges between its normative and empirical aspects. Often times, *fāiā* is confined strictly to family and friends. In that regard, it promotes self-interest and personal gains. In a communal setting, *fāiā* can encourage the shirking of responsibility, and also lead to unclear lines of ac-

---

[4] Taxation of all church ministers is now law as of June 2017: Joyetter Feagaimaalii-Luamanu, "Samoa Head of State Approves Law to Tax Himself, Church Ministers," *Samoa Observer*, 3 July 2017. As of the writing of this paper, all churches have complied except the Congregational Christian Church Samoa (CCCS).

[5] When speaking of the role of the church in Samoa, this paper refers mainly to the context of the Congregational Christian Church Samoa (CCCS).

[6] I am mindful that the context of the CCCS is not representative of the Samoan context. Nevertheless, I am using the term *Samoan context* here in the general sense, for example, as one would think of the Samoan culture referring to the culture in a general sense.

[7] The formative phrase suggests that the construction does not constitute an ancient or old practice. On this see foreword by Jione Havea in Vaitusi Nofoaiga, *A Samoan Reading of Discipleship in Matthew*, IVBS (Atlanta: SBL Press, 2017), x. In this essay, it is a word-construction established to explore the biblical text from a Samoan cultural perspective.

[8] George Pratt, *Pratt's Grammar Dictionary and Samoan Language* (Apia: Malua Printing Press, 1911), 126.

countability. *Fāiā* as used in this paper, though, signifies the existence of an interconnectedness that holds everything together, for better or for worse. It is a holistic approach that embodies all rhetorical and human relations, perceived from my location as a Samoan living in a hybrid world.[9] It is adaptive and bears responsibility and respect for one another, regardless of status or standings in society. It recognizes and acknowledges the presence of the other in a face-to-face configuration.

Upu-ma-fatua'iupu: Making Connections Between Text and Reality

Upu (word, text, speech, language) underscores the usefulness of language, the words used, and the different parts of speech.[10] *Fatua'iupu*[11] (keepers of myths) is the repository of traditional knowledge including chants, songs, and other traditional compositions.[12] A critical aspect of *fatua'iupu* is recognizing the "existence and power of change" on language and culture, and for people to adapt accordingly.[13] The *fatua'iupu*, while showing tolerance to change, insists on connecting it to "life justification proof, the life sources or *lagisoifua*."[14] Connecting one's reading of the text to reality is crucial to the institution of *fatua'iupu*.

Fatua'iupu is made up of two words—*upu* and *fatua'i* (to construct). *Fatua'i* comes from the root word *fatu* (heart, core). The sense is to compose or to construct, "to lay up in the memory, or to compose and commit to memory."[15] This suggests a process of memorization, bridging time and space to ensure the maintenance and sustenance of language and culture. In this regard, *fatua'iupu* signals fluidity and dynamism, recognizing that knowledge and language traverse space and time. To complete the *fāiā*, the joining conjunction *ma* (and)

---

[9] This is something I will discuss more when I talk about my location later in the paper.
[10] Pratt, *Pratt's Grammar*, 72.
[11] According to Samoan tradition, *fatua'iupu* was the name given to the descendants of chief Tauanu'u of the Manu'a islands in Samoa, who was appointed by the Tui Manu'a (King of Manu'a) to be the keeper of traditions for the King. See T. Powell and J. Fraser, "The Samoan Story of Creation: A 'Tala,'" *The Journal of the Polynesian Society* 1.3 (1892): 164–89, cited in Albert Refiti, "Mavae and Tofiga: Spatial Exposition of the Samoan Cosmogony and Architecture" (PhD diss., School of Art & Design, Auckland University of Technology, 2015), 53. In modern days, the term *Fatua'iupu* is often employed in association with efforts in government and educational institutions to revive and preserve Samoan traditions and language.
[12] Refiti, "Mavae and Tofiga," 52; Fanaafi Le Tagaloa Aiono, *O Motugaafa* (Alafua, USP: Le Lamepa Press, 1996).
[13] Aiono, *O Motugaafa*, 2.
[14] Aiono, *O Motugaafa*, 2.
[15] Pratt, *Pratt's Grammar*, 137.

bridges the two isolated entities of *upu* and *fatua'iupu*.[16] On the whole, the *fāiā-i-upu-ma-fatua'iupu* (hereinafter referred to as *fāiā* approach), connotes exploring relations and connections in words, word constructions, and meaning.

Fāiā Approach: Symbolic of My Location

My use of the *fāiā* approach is symbolic of my location. I exist in a world of *fāiā* (interconnectedness), a product of both western thinking and of Samoan values and beliefs. I was born and raised in Samoa, supported by institutions including the church, family, and community that facilitated my coming into being, shaping how I relate to others. This sense of *fāiā* assumed a different form having lived in the United States throughout my adult life. My experience working in the US Congress, an institution characterized by political gridlock and stalemate, has taught me the value and/or necessity of dialogue, compromise, and finding common grounds. Diverse interests, both at the national and at the constituent level, warrant building relations. Minding relations necessitates massaging differences and highlighting similarities.[17] In this manner, I see myself as someone occupying a third space in a hybrid world.[18] My worldview warrants negotiating the boundaries of who I am, my experience, and my westernized education. My location within this third space inspires me to employ the *fāiā* approach, a product of my own struggle to integrate my Samoan-ness and my westernized education.[19] My framework is similar to Vaitusi Nofoaiga's *tautuaileva* (service that is rendered at a place that is in-between) approach.[20] In *tautuaileva*, Nofoaiga integrates the world of the text, the Samoan context, and the academic world, to bear on discipleship. While Nofoaiga refers to this as *va* (engagement), I prefer *fāiā* instead. *Fāiā* explores possible connections, even where there is silence or space in the text, exploring ways to bridge the world behind the text, the world of the text, and the world in front of the text.

---

[16] "Ma" can also be translated as shame, or embarrassment, but it is used here for its bridging aspects, as a joining conjunction.

[17] The idea of "massage" draws from the Samoan concept of *fofō*, or in particular in the process of birthing. The Samoan *fofō* (masseuse) *fofō* the belly of the mother so that the baby in the womb is properly aligned. The idea is to negotiate and massage to make the whole process of giving birth safe and comfortable for the mother and the baby. This is the whole idea behind the use of *fofō*, to negotiate and manage challenges in the process.

[18] Homi K. Bhabha, *The Location of Culture* (New York: Routledge 1994), 36–38.

[19] Nofoaiga *A Samoan Reading*, 165 also talks about the limitations of hybridity. In response, perhaps the impure aspects of hybridity bespeak the sense of multiplicity of perspectives and that there is no one pure view. From this location there is a continuing process of negotiation.

[20] Nofoaiga, *A Samoan Reading*.

Despite the potential of other methodological approaches, I use sociorhetorical interpretation for its interdisciplinary and multi-faceted aspects.[21] It allows the interpreter to move "between the world behind the text, the world of or in the text, and the world in front of the text created by contemporary interpretation."[22] Using sociorhetorical interpretation, I explore the *fāiā* embedded in the language of the text, to examine how they shape and create meaning in order to make the text more meaningful in my context. Sociorhetorical interpretation provides the platform to bridge my context and the text, while engaging in dialogue with other contemporary thinkers.

Fāiā within the Inner Texture of Romans 13:1–7

One of the main subjects of interest appears to be the noun ἐξουσία.[23] The sense of ἐξουσία suggests a "bearer of ruling authority"[24] or the notion of "those persons who have the authority to rule or govern."[25] While the focus is on the bearer of authority, it does not stipulate legitimacy, nor the right to interpret laws, or cause someone to be under the authority of someone else.[26] The emphasis, though, is on the *fāiā* to θεός. All six occurrences of "God" (NRSV) indicate some sort of *fāiā* to those in authority. In verse 1, God is the source of authority. In verse 2, those in authority are appointed by God, and in verses 4 and 5, they are servants of God.

From a *fāiā* perspective, Rom 13:1 represents the opening of the rhetorical unit, introducing the *fāiā* between the Roman audience and the governing authorities. The heart of the *fāiā* resides in the assertion that God is sovereign. Without God, there is no *fāiā*. The nature of the *fāiā*, though, is more complex and nuanced. Submission is qualified by other considerations including the

---

[21] I am mindful that others like Ben Witherington III use the term sociorhetorical but with a different meaning. This paper is based on Vernon Robbins's sociorhetorical approach.
[22] Elaine Wainwright, "Reading Matthew 3–4: Jesus-Sage, Seer, Sophia, Son of God," *JSNT* 77 (2000): 29.
[23] I am aware that there was some scholarly debate whether ἐξουσία in verse 3 also refers to angelic powers: Susan Boyer, "Exegesis of Romans 13:1–7," *Brethren Life and Thought* 32 (1987): 208–16. I concur with both Boyer and Robert H. Stein, "The Argument of Romans 13:1–7," *NovT* 31 (1989): 325–43, that Paul here is referring to earthly authorities. It is only in the disputed Pauline letters that one finds reference to the invisible powers. Moreover, the connection between authorities and taxation in verse 6 is a strong indication that ἐξουσία refers to earthly authority.
[24] According to BDAG, s.v. "ἐξουσία," ἐξουσία has a wide range of meaning in early Christian literature, including "authority," "right," "power," or "official."
[25] Jan Botha, *Subject to Whose Authority? Multiple Readings of Romans 13*, ESEC 4 (Atlanta: Scholars Press, 1994), 42.
[26] Botha, *Subject to Whose Authority*, 42–43.

"form of human government in which one resides."[27] The inference can be drawn that "voluntary submission to authority is also qualified submission."[28] It is not a command for blind obedience. Submission is due to the earthly authorities if they are just and righteous. In other words, to say that the *faiā* between authorities and subjects demands absolute obedience "is to violate the meaning of the text."[29]

The ambivalent nature of the text suggests that even though a relationship exists between government and subjects, the nature of this relationship is subject to other factors, other possible *faiā*. The text does not define a particular role for the church community in Rome. To demand absolute obedience or blatantly call for resistance is to define a particular response. Rather, the text exemplifies the difficulties in navigating the complex social, cultural, and ideological *faiā* among the Roman audience. It is a reminder of the complexities and totality of the community, and the implication this may have on the *faiā* between governing authorities and subjects.

The strategic placement of the inferential conjunction in verse 2 is crucial to the middle of the passage—verse 2 through verse 4. The inferential conjunction ὥστε introduces an independent clause logically based on the preceding statement in verse 1.[30] Subsequently, verses 3 and 4 provide further evidence in support of the independent clause in verse 2. In turn, the middle segment shows support for the *faiā* connecting the church community in Rome and the governing authorities.

Similarly, the placement of the inferential conjunction διό in verse 5 signals the closing segment from verse 5 through verse 7. The flow of the argument moves from a single *faiā* to a broader context, suggesting other relationships. Paul D. Feinberg notes that the relation between verse 6 and the preceding verses is unclear.[31] Even verse 7 appears appended, and is more closely related to the latter verses from verse 8 through verse 14.[32] I agree with James D. G. Dunn that there is enough evidence to support that both verse 6 and verse 7 are connected

---

[27] Joseph Fitzmyer, *Romans: A New Translation with Introduction and Commentary*, AB 33 (New York: Doubleday, 1993), 665.

[28] William R. Herzog II, "Dissembling, a Weapon of the Weak: The Case of Christ and Caesar in Mark 12:13–17 and Romans 13:1–7," *Perspectives in Religious Studies* 21 (1994): 339–60.

[29] Alexander F. C. Webster, "St. Paul's Political Advice to the Haughty Gentile Christians in Rome: An Exegesis of Romans 13:1–7," *St Vladimir's Theological Quarterly* 25 (1981): 269.

[30] Jon Nelson Bailey, "Paul's Political Paraenesis in Romans 13:1–7," *Restoration Quarterly* 46 (2004): 18.

[31] Paul D. Feinberg, "The Christian and Civil Authorities." *Master's Seminary Journal* 10 (1999): 96.

[32] Bruce J. Malina and John J. Pilch, *Social-Science Commentary on the Letters of Paul* (Minneapolis: Fortress, 2006), 281.

to the preceding verses.[33] I would add, however, that the rhetorical unit overall suggests a sophisticated *fāiā* framework, one that takes into consideration the various challenges facing the Roman audience.

Fāiā and the Progressive Texture of Romans 13:1–7

Memorization and remembrance are critical aspects from a *fāiā* perspective, especially to a listening Roman audience. In this regard, there is a *fāiā* between Rom 13:1–7 and its immediate literary context. In 13:5 for example, ὀργή and συνείδησις appear to be the qualifying agents. Obedience to the governing authorities is weighed upon by "wrath" (NRSV) and "conscience" (NRSV). Those who subject themselves to the governing authorities do so not because of fear, but from a reasoned position.[34] This is preceded by 12:2 in which the readers are cautioned not to be "conformed to this world, but be transformed by the renewing of your minds" (NRSV). The aim is to "discern what is the will of God—what is good and acceptable and perfect." Later in 12:19, the text encourages the audience not to seek revenge, "but leave room for the wrath of God" (NRSV). The sense is that God will see to it that the wrong done will be repaid. Read against 12:2 and 12:19, the tone in Rom 13:1–7 softens.

Romans 13, therefore, can be seen as a *fāiā* between chapters 12 and 14. Susan Boyer sees in this progression a call "for Christian citizenship" rather than affirming a divine basis for government authority.[35] The relationship between members of the Roman churches and the governing authorities is qualified by other considerations such as one's discernment of God's will, allowing God to make judgment, and even welcoming everyone including the "weak in faith" (NRSV) in 14:1. The effect is to suggest a sophisticated relational framework that nurtures and sustains healthy relationships among members of a community. In this regard, Rom 13:1–7 is ambiguous as it anticipates and negotiates diverse *fāiā* within the community.[36]

---

[33] James D. G. Dunn, "Romans 13.1–7: A Charter for Political Quietism?," *Ex Auditu* 2 (1986): 62.
[34] Sze-Kar Wan, "Coded Resistance: Rereading Romans 13:1–7," in *The Bible in the Public Square: Reading the Signs of the Times*, ed. Cynthia Briggs Kittredge, Ellen Bradshaw Aitken, and Jonathan A. Draper (Minneapolis: Fortress, 2008), 178.
[35] Boyer, "Exegesis of Romans 13:1–7," 211.
[36] Emanuel Gerrit Singgih, "Towards a Post Colonial Interpretation of Romans 13:1–7: Karl Barth, Robert Jewett and the Context of Reformation in Present-Day Indonesia," *Asia Journal of Theology* 23 (2009): 121.

Fāiā within the Argumentative Texture

So far in the argument, the text underscores a *fāiā* between God and authority. This single and pivotal *fāiā* forms the basis for all other *fāiā*. Subsequently, the flow of the argument in the middle segment reveals other plausible *fāiā*. As God provides the basis for all authorities, the supporting statement assumes a *fāiā* with κρίμα which signals both "the threat of facing God's tribunal, as well as governmental verdicts."[37] It has both the sense of God's judgment and of government verdict. Verse 3 also mentions ἄρχων.[38] This gives the sense that "the person or persons in question are those who are responsible for the relationship between two parties" in which one rules or governs the other.[39] The focus is on the person. From a *fāiā* perspective, there is a *fāiā* that connects κρίμα, ἀγαθὸν ἔργον, and κακός in verse 3. The connection continues the logical progression from the main assertion that God is authority and that submission to all other authorities is warranted because of God's supreme authority. As a derivative of that premise, God also gives judgment—judgment on both good and bad conduct. In other words, the mention of both good and bad conduct suggests an important relational matter. It is quite possible from a *fāiā* perspective that the logical progression of the argument suggests human relations within the church community in Rome. In this regard, the rhetorical connection in the text reflects the dynamics of human relations among the audience.

In the closing segment of the text, more *fāiā* emerge. A connection can be established between conscience, wrath, taxes, and honor, although its nature and contours are not defined. Because the authority "bears the sword" (13:4, NRSV), it is easy to see the connection between submitting to government and wrath. The interesting connection, however, is with conscience. Based on the pivotal assertion that God is supreme authority and provides the basis of all authorities, the supporting statement is to submit to the authorities out of συνείδησις. This is the "middle-step" of discernment that Jon Isaak argues "involves reflection and assessment."[40] The question, though, is what standard is to be used to inform moral decisions. From a *fāiā* perspective, the connection between Rom 13:1–7 and its immediate literary context is important. The use of conscience coupled with discernment and thoughtful deliberation in 12:2 softens the call to submit to

---

[37] κρίμα has within its semantic range "justice," "decree," or "verdict," BDAG, s.v. "κρίμα." See Robert Jewett, *Romans: A Commentary* (Minneapolis: Fortress, 2007), 792.

[38] ἄρχων has within its range of meanings "ruler" or "governor." See Botha, *Subject to Whose Authority*, 44.

[39] Botha, *Subject to Whose Authority*, 44.

[40] Jon Isaak, "The Christian Community and Political Responsibility: Romans 13:1–7," *Direction* 32 (2003): 41–42.

governing authorities.[41] It renders a somewhat fluid relationship between Christians and the governing authorities that underscores an "assessing discernment amidst 'conflicting thoughts'" leaving the door open to "conscientious disobedience or selective obedience."[42] In other words, conscience underscores the fluid and malleable nature of the *fāiā* between government and subjects and it leaves open the opportunity for discernment with respect to obedience.

A rhetorical connection exists also between συνείδησις in verse 5, and the φόρος in verse 6.[43] In this instance, the likely sense of φόρος, which also appears in verse 7, points to taxation. The text underscores the sensitivity of taxation as an issue. Similarly, a rhetorical connection exists between συνείδησις and τέλος in verse 7, which in this instance is a generic term for a wide range of government import and use taxes.[44] From a *fāiā* perspective, the text highlights the connection between the exhortation to submit and the issue of taxation. Together with the rhetorical connection between συνείδησις in verse 5 and τιμή in verse 7, these connections are made possible through the Greek phrase διὰ τοῦτο γάρ in verse 6 which references the discussion on συνείδησις in verse 5.[45] Similarly, a rhetorical connection exists between συνείδησις and φόβος which has within its semantic range "intimidation," "terror," "respect," or "fear."[46] From a *fāiā* perspective, there is a connection between one's decision to pay everything owed, conscience, and respect. The challenge is in navigating the nuances of anticipated *fāiā*.

Fāiā in the Social and Cultural Texture of the Text

From a *fāiā* perspective, it can be argued that Rom 13:1–7 is in the form of challenge-response, a *fāiā* in itself.[47] It is the *fāiā* between Paul and the church community in Rome, a relationship in which one stimulates and the recipient responds.[48] The text represents a challenge from Paul, who is seeking to share in

---

[41] Helene Dorothea Bertschmann, "Bowing before Christ—Nodding to the State? Reading Paul Politically with Oliver O' Donovan and John Howard Yoder" (PhD diss., University of Durham, 2012), 165.
[42] Pol Vonck, "All Authority Comes from God: Romans 13:1–7: A Tricky Text About Obedience to Political Power," *African Ecclesial Review* 26 (1984): 343.
[43] φόρος has the meaning of "tribute" or "tax," BDAG, s.v. "φόρος."
[44] Jewett, *Romans*, 802.
[45] τιμή is understood to have the meaning of "honor." See Stein, "The Argument of Romans 13:1–7," 342.
[46] BDAG, s.v. "φόβος."
[47] Note here that Bruce Malina, whom Robbins is quoting verbatim, uses the term challenge-riposte, and Robbins acknowledges this. Robbins primarily uses the term challenge-response in his work but maintains the same meaning and application.
[48] Vernon K. Robbins, *Exploring the Texture of the Texts: A Guide to Socio-rhetorical Interpretation* (Harrisburg, PA: Trinity Press International, 1996), 80, explains that a

the space occupied by his audience, and share also their resources in support of his mission to Spain. The text seeks to bring together a community that is still developing an identity as a group, and also divided because of diverse social, cultural, and ideological backgrounds. As Yeo Khiok-khng writes, "relationships within these ethnically, ideologically, and religiously mixed congregations had produced conflicts."[49] A certain degree of complexity, therefore, exists among the church community in Rome. From a sociorhetorical perspective, Paul is here introducing, developing, and nurturing wisdom in the community. For Paul, then, the challenge is to navigate the confluence of views and massage differences that exist among his readers. Bringing together the divided community warrants an approach that is cognizant of existing *fāiā*.

In this regard, there is a correlation between the ambiguous nature of the text and the multilayered relation between Paul's audience and the governing authorities. Sze-Kar Wan argues that this is due to Paul talking in coded language, intended to be understood at two levels.[50] On one level, the text is for "public consumption," aiming at the "calculating logic of the dominant class." On another level, it is for "the underclass in Roman society." Roland Boer also suggests that because of the imposing Roman empire, Paul is "two-faced" and undecided between "a choice of opposing or accommodating."[51] I argue however in support of a more sophisticated Paul.

From a *fāiā* perspective, Paul is massaging and consoling existing confrontational and convoluted social, cultural, and political lines. In so doing, the text is purposefully ambiguous. On one hand, the exhortation to submit reflects a challenge to those who are more inclined to resist government. Paul may have been very well aware of a "rising tide of zealotry in Palestine" when crafting Rom 13:1–7.[52] In this regard, the image of the sword wielding servant of God serves as deterrent.

---

challenge-response constitutes a challenge which can be in the form of "word." The word underscores a challenge to share in the social space of another and for purposes that are mutually cooperative. In this case, I argue that Romans not only introduces Paul to his readers, but also seeks their cooperation and support for Paul's intended mission to Spain. Seeking a favorable and cooperative response from the audience warrants being sensitive to the diverse and multilayer of relations among the church community.

[49] Yeo Khiok-khng, "Introduction: Navigating Romans through Cultures," in *Navigating Romans through Cultures: Challenging Readings by Charting a New Course*, ed. Yeo Khiok-khng (K. K.) (New York: T&T Clark International, 2004), 12.

[50] Wan, "Coded Resistance," 179.

[51] Roland Boer, "Resistance Versus Accommodation: What to Do with Romans 13?," *Postcolonial Interventions: Essays in Honor of R. S. Sugirtharajah*, ed. Tat-Siong Benny Liew (Sheffield: Sheffield Phoenix, 2009), 119–20.

[52] Harold J. Dyck, "The Christian and the Authorities in Romans 13:1–7," *Direction* 14 (1985): 48.

On the other hand, there may have been others who were also enjoying the perks of submitting to governing authorities. In a society deeply immersed in patron-client relationships, any association or connections with governing authorities were highly sought.[53] From a *fāiā approach*, therefore, the text is sensitive to the diverse political tendencies among the readers. It underscores an effort to massage and console a very delicate position within the community in Rome. Through the text, we are led to think of Paul as politically savvy and strategically sensitive to the existing *fāiā* among his audience members.

Feagai-ga: Rethinking the *Fāiā* between Church and State in Samoa

The word *feagai-ga* comes from the root word *feagai*, which has a range of meanings including "to be opposite to each other," "to correspond," or "to dwell together cordially."[54] The nuances of meaning seem to converge on the point that *feagai* suggests facing one another.[55] As a noun, therefore, the word *feagai-ga* conveys the sense that the involved parties are engaged in a face-to-face configuration. It is this sense of *feagai-ga* that gives meaning to other social configurations such as the relation between *mātua* and *fānau* (parents-children), or *tama fafine* and *tama tane* (brothers-sisters). Perhaps this is why the word *feagaiga* is also understood to have the meaning of "covenant," which in essence is the mutual recognition of certain roles and responsibilities within a particular accord.[56] Because of its use to signify a treaty or covenant, the word *feagaiga*, however, has become confined and limited.

Using the *fāiā* approach, the text in Rom 13:1–7, though, underscores a framework that reorients the church and governing authorities in a *feagai-ga* or face-to-face configuration. In its basic sense, it implies fluidity. The nature and dynamics of the relation are abstract and fragile. Responsibility and respect are warranted, recognizing the value in one another.

Feagai-ga, moreover, values the *va tapuia* (the space in between), as sacred.[57] The ambiguity in the text embodies this space in between. It conveys an

---

[53] Botha, "Subject to Whose Authority?," 214.
[54] Notice the construction of a hyphenated "*feagai-ga*" to distinguish it from *feagaiga*, which has become synonymous with "covenant." My purpose is to differentiate between the two, arguing instead for an interpretation of *feagai-ga* which signals infinite roles and functions. On *feagaiga* see Pratt, *Pratt's Grammar*, 139.
[55] I had an opportunity to discuss this with Tui Atua Tupua Tamasese Efi in 2017. Efi's emphasis was on the face-to-face configuration that underscores the word *feagai*. In this way, *feagai* is the verb that suggests sitting opposite each other. Adding the suffix *ga* results in the word becoming a noun. Thus, *feagai-ga* is a noun which suggests a face-to-face configuration.
[56] Pratt, *Pratt's Grammar*, 139.
[57] A lot of Pacific scholars discuss this as space, the sacred space symbolic of the relationship in-between. Nofoaiga, *A Samoan Reading*, also touches on this concept of space,

understanding that while there is a *fāiā*, the text is malleable enough to allow freedom and space to operate. It is undefined and infinite, allowing movement, adjustments, and realignment. In this regard, to intrude into the *va tapuia* is to disrespect the *fāiā*, the *feagai-ga*. Maintaining a fluid and dynamic relation is crucial. It is in a way, a very sophisticated arrangement that calls for the capacity to adapt and to reflect.

Given the recent turn of events, a rethinking of the relationship between church and state in Samoa is in order. The church is becoming marginalized. Much of this marginalization, ironically, is due to the church's own preoccupation with the cultural designation of *feagaiga*. This cultural designation has resulted in the church being accorded the highest status in Samoan society. It has also effectively placed the church outside of the political realm, insulated from issues that matter. Put in other words, it is fair to say that this is a form of "privileged marginalization." By virtue of its privileged designation, the church is in fact marginalized in terms of what it can and cannot do in society, becoming institutionalized and stagnant over time.

Observations for Further Discussion

This rereading of Rom 13:1–7 in the context of church and state relations in Samoa has provided the opportunity to make some critical observations. In my analysis, I find considerable evidence to suggest the validity of the following observations.

Observation 1. The existence of *fāiā* within the text of Rom 13:1–7 suggests that the text was deliberately crafted to allow space and freedom for movement.

Romans 13:1–7 does not constitute a defined Christian response. The existence of several *fāiā* or connections gives rise to ambiguities in the text. The imperative to subject oneself, for example, is weighed upon by conscience. Conscience acts as a disclaimer, suggesting that subjection is not absolute. Both wrath and conscience obviate absolute obedience to government, allowing the church community space. The intended effect is for a more fluid role. In other words, multiple rhetorical connections within the text suggest richness in meaning and interpretation. And while it may have been written for a particular context, the ambiguous nature of the text has made it meaningful across time and context.[58] From this perspective, Rom 13:1–7 underwrites an intriguing Christian political thought and response. It is first and foremost a statement about the need for the

---

or as he calls it, *va* or engagement. See Aiono, *O Motugaafa*, 25, also for her discussion of *va-tapuia*.

[58] Webster, "St. Paul's Political Advice," 260.

church to be reflective and adaptive rather than becoming institutionalized and static.

Observation 2. The ambiguity in Rom 13:1–7 suggests much about the relationships and dynamics among the church community in Rome.

The nature and characteristic of the church community in Rome remains an area of scholarly debate.[59] Because Paul in Romans quotes from the Old Testament frequently, many scholars have argued this is evidence that his readers were primarily of Jewish background.[60] Joseph A. Fitzmyer notes several references to gentiles within the text of Romans, which strongly suggests a significant proportion of Paul's readers were of gentile background. The Roman church accordingly was "a mixed community, partly of Jewish, but predominantly of Gentile background."[61]

Wolfgang Wiefel's account of the historical events leading to the formation of the Roman church is also evidentiary.[62] For Wiefel, tracing the origin of the Roman church starts with Emperor Claudius's edict expelling the Jewish population from Rome.[63] This historical event signaled the end of the first Christian congregation in Rome, which up until then had been primarily constituted by Jewish Christians. The expulsion of the Jewish people from Rome created space for gentile Christians to take over the new community.[64] This new community began to organize itself around church houses rather than synagogues.[65] As a result, the emerging Roman church effectively consisted of several house churches, perhaps also with house owners of totally disparate political affinities. It is quite plausible then that some pro-government sentiments may have developed among the gentile Christians. When the Jewish Christians returned around 54 CE, there would have been some disparate attitudes and responses towards the government.

Against this historical setting, assertions can be made about the ambiguous nature of Rom 13. Some scholars, like Sung U. Lim, argue that in Rom 13 Paul crafted a section that underscores a double-voice, one with a public agenda and

---

[59] Victor Manuel Morales Vasquez, *Contours of Biblical Reception Theory: Studies in the Rezeptionsgeschichte of Romans 13.1–7* (Göttingen: V & R Unipress, 2012), 111.
[60] Fitzmyer, *Romans*, 32.
[61] Fitzmyer, *Romans*, 32.
[62] Wolfgang Wiefel, "The Jewish Community in Ancient Rome and the Origins of Roman Christians (Revised and Expanded)," in *The Romans Debate*, ed. Karl P. Donfried (Peabody, MA: Hendrickson Publishers 1991), 85–101.
[63] Wiefel, "The Jewish Community," 93.
[64] Wiefel, "The Jewish Community," 94.
[65] Wiefel, "The Jewish Community," 95.

one a hidden agenda.[66] In a sense, Paul recognizes the presence of both antiimperial and proimperial views in his audience. Boer instead notes that contradictions and ambiguities are characteristics of Paul's writings. In the case of Rom 13:1–7 Paul is tasked with navigating different socioeconomic systems, a task in which "the realms of thought, theology and writing are not divorced from their historical context, especially their socioeconomic context."[67] For Dunn, the "central factor" for understanding Rom 13 "is the ambiguous and vulnerable status" of the Jewish people.[68]

The evidence from my study lends evidence to the argument that the ambiguous nature of the text is largely a factor of the various *fāiā* among the church community in Rome. Paul was tasked with navigating a volatile social, cultural, ideological, and political environment. The text embodies a certain sensitivity to the diverse political thoughts and responses among Paul's readers. In writing to gain support for his trip to Spain, it was more important to Paul that he show sensitivity to what is important to the church community. In other words, the text reveals Paul as politically astute as well as sensitive to the plurality and diversity of his readers.

In an increasingly diverse and emerging community, Paul offers a framework pivotal to establishing and minding relations, a *feagai-ga* relational framework. With God as the linchpin, Paul presents a framework fitting for a community with thriving and developing relations among its members. In a *feagai-ga* relational framework, Paul also extends a model to strengthen relations among a community still in flux and living within the shadow of imperial power.

Observation 3. Ambiguities in Rom 13:1–7 allow for a Christian political thought and response that relativizes power and control, and elevates respect and love in all relations.

I find evidence in the study to suggest the validity of the observation that the ambiguities in Rom 13 obviate power and control in all relations. From a *fāiā* perspective, the process of remembering is key. Based on the assumption that the letter is to be read to the audience, there are several *fāiā* tying 13:1–7 to its immediate literary context. In his navigating of the many *fāiā* among his Roman audience, Paul in effect crafts a statement which, in light of its immediate literary context, can be understood as elevating the need for love and respect in all relations. Scholars like Dean Pinter, for example, argue that chapters 12–15 are

---

[66] Sung U. Lim, "A Double-Voiced Reading of Romans 13:1–7 in Light of the Imperial Cult," *HTS Teologiese/Theological Studies* (*HvTSt*) 71(1) (2015): art. 2475, doi.org/10.4102/hts.v71i1.2475.
[67] Boer, "Resistance Versus Accommodation," 116.
[68] Dunn, "Romans 13.1–7," 58.

to "guide the somewhat divided Roman church toward Christian unity as they learn to love one another."[69] Romans 13:1–7 presents a framework that puts less emphasis on status, allowing space for movement and fluidity in the nature of the relationship. Rather than imposing finite roles and limited responsibilities, the text suggests instead a *fāiā* framework based on love and respect for one another, building bridges rather than being divisive and exclusive.

In light of the recent developments in Samoa it is the contention of this paper that the *feagai-ga* reading of Rom 13 suggests an alternative—for the church to be adaptive and reflective. It is not a call for absolute obedience, nor a blatant call for resistance against government. Rather, being adaptive and reflective sustains God's will for the church to be the prophetic voice in society, the voice of the marginalized, fighting against injustice in society. Because it is not bounded by limited expectations and restricted roles, the *feagai-ga* orientation allows the church space to freely respond in the interest of fulfilling God's will. It prevents the church from becoming static and institutionalized, risking it losing relevancy against forces of globalization and modernization. In this regard, it is plausible that the ongoing taxation dispute offers an inflexion point for the church. No longer is the church to be sidelined from policy considerations affecting the lives of the people, but to be the voice of the poor and those who are disenfranchised by the unmitigated authority of government. The church in Samoa perhaps stands as a glimmer of hope, providing checks and balances to sustain a fragile democracy in a single-party government system.

Conclusion

This study offers an alternative reading of Rom 13:1–7 using an approach that includes the analysis of the text and applies a hermeneutical lens to read the text. While the framework appears to be a two-part undertaking, between analysis and interpretation, separating the two is not always clear and clean. The analysis and interpretation are often simultaneously carried out and connected.

As indicated at the outset, the goal for this study is to use a Samoan concept to analyze the text, and as a reading lens to make sense of Rom 13:1–7 from my context. It is based on a worldview borne of my experience living in the Samoan diaspora. In this regard, the hyphenated *feagai-ga*, and the *fāiā* approach are symbolic of how I see myself. I occupy a place that warrants taking into consideration multiple perspectives, finding connections between different and diverse worldviews. Moreover, I see the Samoan culture as not static or defined, but as a living entity. From this location, I try to bridge the world of the text and the

---

[69] Dean Pinter, "Josephus and Romans 13:1–14: Providence and Imperial Power," in *Reading Romans in Context: Paul and Second Temple Judaism*, ed. Ben C. Blackwell, John K. Goodrich, and Jason Maston (Grand Rapids, MI: Zondervan, 2015), 146.

world of other scholars, to focus on Rom 13:1–7 by engaging in dialogue with the relationship between church and state in Samoa. It is a Samoan-based methodological approach, integrated with aspects of sociorhetorical interpretation.

Three observations regarding Rom 13:1–7 are offered. The evidence from the study suggests the validity of these observations for further research and the need to continue the dialogue. While using a particular context might not be ground for valid generalizations, the aim is to generate observations for more *talanoa* (discussion).

Finally, I am mindful that in today's political environment the search for answers and resolutions often necessitates definitive and less ambiguous responses. From a *fāiā* perspective, the biblical text is to be read and understood as living and adaptive to social, cultural, and political changes over time. In this regard, the biblical text offers space for movement. Perhaps the perspective also recognizes that in our continuous search for answers and determinations we may ignore the fact that there may be a multiple rather than single answer. In this way, our responses are not dangled as absolute but negotiable. Minding our interconnectedness allows respect for one another, meanwhile making way into the abyss of spaces and voids within our midst.

Part 3
Explorations in Africa and Asia

Intersectional Texture: Reconsidering Gender Critical Frameworks and Sociorhetorical Interpretation

Johnathan Jodamus

Introduction

Vernon K. Robbins, in his chapter of the book *Rhetoric, Ethic and Moral Persuasion in Biblical Discourse*, ends with the following question regarding rhetorical biblical interpretation: "Don't you wonder what people might say in 2022? That, of course, will be thirty years after the 1992 Heidelberg conference!"[1] The 1994 Pretoria conference, which was the second of seven Pepperdine conferences initiated by Thomas H. Olbricht, was one of many rhetoric conferences hosted in South Africa in the early 1990's by an almost exclusively white and male biblical studies guild, with the dawn of democracy clearly within view. Apart from the now infamous debate that emerged from those conferences between Elisabeth Schüssler Fiorenza and Robbins,[2] what was

---

[1] Vernon K. Robbins, "From Heidelberg to Heidelberg: Rhetorical Interpretation of the Bible at the Seven 'Pepperdine' Conferences from 1992 to 2002," in *Rhetoric, Ethic, and Moral Persuasion in Biblical Discourse: Essays from the 2002 Heidelberg Conference*, ed. Thomas H. Olbricht and Anders Eriksson, ESEC 11 (London: T&T Clark, 2005), 377.

[2] Elisabeth Schüssler Fiorenza, "Challenging the Rhetorical Half-Turn: Feminist and Rhetorical Biblical Criticism," in *Rhetoric, Scripture and Theology: Essays from the 1994 Pretoria Conference*, ed. Stanley E. Porter and Thomas H. Olbricht, JSNTSup 131 (Sheffield: Sheffield Academic, 1996), 28–53; Vernon K. Robbins, "The Rhetorical Full-Turn in Biblical Interpretation: Reconfiguring Rhetorical-Political Analysis," in *Rhetorical Criticism and the Bible*, ed. Stanley E. Porter and Dennis L. Stamps, JSNTSup 195 (Sheffield: Sheffield Academic, 2002), 49–60; Robbins, "The Rhetorical Full-Turn in Biblical Interpretation and Its Relevance for Feminist Hermeneutics," in *Her Master's Tools?*, ed. Caroline Vander Stichele and Todd Penner, GPBS 9 (Atlanta: Society of Biblical Literature; Leiden: Brill, 2005), 109–27; Priscilla Geisterfer, "Full Turns and Half

largely absent from the debates was the fact that the additional conferences on rhetoric in South Africa also were almost exclusively attended and organized by white male South African biblical scholars. The invitation to write this article, therefore, makes me feel like I embody a response to the essays in *Foundations for Sociorhetorical Exploration* through my very presence as an author of an essay in this volume entitled *Welcoming the Nations*. I am a relatively young, emerging black academic in South Africa engaging in a study of ancient sacred texts, while the guild of biblical scholars in South Africa remains, more than two decades later, largely white and male, judging from my participation over the past seven years in the New Testament Society of Southern Africa. In this context it is my pleasure to respond with some thoughts on the shape of the discourse around sociorhetorical interpretation (SRI) in the wider global academy, and more specifically in my own South African context as a cis-gendered, heterosexual black man.

Reflections on My SRI Journey

What I offer in this contribution are some preliminary considerations, which I hope to develop in greater detail later, regarding the utility of SRI for critical theory in general, and gender critical theory in particular. These thoughts are borne out of a great deal of recent reflection on my journey of utilizing SRI first in my masters thesis, then as a key analytic in my PhD dissertation.[3] More recently, I have also been teaching graduate courses incorporating SRI and gender frameworks, and the debates referred to above, which ostensibly place gender at the center, to the exclusion of race, class, and politics. In the volumes emerging from the rhetoric conferences, the proverbial elephant in the room is the glaring absence of black voices and their reflections on the political context of South Africa at the time. Notwithstanding Schüssler Fiorenza's appeal in some of these publications to consider the nexus of race, class, gender, and coloniality, her reflections seem to remain at a disembodied level.

These critical reflections on the conferences held in my context bring me to expand and perhaps reconsider what I believe to be a major advance in a new application of SRI deployed through a gender-critical lens in my PhD dissertation. I believe this advance has implications for how SRI is conceptualized and practiced. In my dissertation I brought a blending of SRI and gender-critical

---

Turns: Engaging the Dialogue/Dance between Elisabeth Schüssler Fiorenza and Vernon Robbins," in Stichele and Penner, *Her Master's Tools?*, 129–44.

[3] Johnathan Jodamus, "A Socio-rhetorical Exegesis of 1 Timothy 2:8–15" (MSocSci thesis, Department of Religious Studies, University of Cape Town, South Africa, 2005). Johnathan Jodamus, "An Investigation into the Construction(s) and Representation(s) of Masculinity(ies) and Femininity(ies) in 1 Corinthians" (PhD diss., University of Cape Town, South Africa, 2015).

interpretive strategies to bear on an investigation of masculinity and femininity in 1 Corinthians.[4] A reading of the gendered-imagery of the Pauline rhetoric demonstrated, I argue, that Paul deploys Greco-Roman tropes of gender/sex in his rhetoric in a dominant, hegemonic, and hierarchical way.

The most important insights offered by my approach are not SRI or gender-critical specific, but come about in the blending of the two, thereby making a contribution to methodological conversations and innovations in the field of New Testament interpretation. By grafting key aspects of gender-theory into the larger framework of identity-construction, I believe that new possibilities for SRI open up. Gender theory as understood through the optic of identity proves to be helpful in shifting away from straight up gender theoretical discussion to the larger issue of the construction of the individual in relation to society, language, and historical context—what some scholars might argue is a thoroughly intersectional approach.

These reflections have led me to a decision to argue in this essay for an additional texture in SRI called *intersectional texture*. In the context of intersectional analysis during the 1980s especially in the work of Patricia Hill Collins, the legal scholar Kimberlé Crenshaw is most frequently credited with coining the term *intersectionality* in her 1989 essay "Demarginalizing the Intersection of Race and Sex."[5] Crenshaw selected the metaphor of "an intersection, coming and going in all four directions" to describe discrimination, which "like traffic through an intersection, may flow in one direction, and it may flow in another. If an accident happens in an intersection, it can be caused by cars traveling from any number of directions and, sometimes, from all of them."[6] Out of these beginning places, which included descriptions of multiple jeopardy and multiple consciousness,[7] a definition of intersectionality has emerged that clarifies the connected relationships among two systems of oppression: intersectionality and the matrix of domination:

> Intersectionality refers to particular forms of intersecting oppressions, for example, intersections of race and gender, or of sexuality and nation. Intersectional paradigms remind us that oppression cannot be reduced to one

---

[4] Jodamus, "An Investigation into the Construction(s) and Representation(s)."
[5] Patricia Hill Collins, *Black Feminist Thought: Knowledge, Empowerment and Consciousness* (New York: Routledge, 2000). Kimberlé W. Crenshaw, "Demargininalizing the Intersection of Race and Sex: A Black Feminist Critique of Antidiscrimination Doctrine, Feminist Theory and Antiracist Politics," *University of Chicago Legal Forum* 140 (1989): 139–67; cf. Crenshaw, "Mapping the Margins: Intersectionality, Identity Politics, and Violence against Women of Color," *Stanford Law Review* 46 (1991): 1241–99, cited in Mary Romero, *Introducing Intersectionality* (Malden, MA: Polity Press, 2018), 39.
[6] Crenshaw, "Demarginalizing the Intersection of Race and Sex," 149.
[7] Deborah King, "Multiple Jeopardy, Multiple Consciousness: The Context of Black Feminist Ideology," *Signs: Journal of Women in Culture and Society* 14 (1988): 88–111.

fundamental type, and that oppressions work together in producing injustice. In contrast, the matrix of domination refers to how these intersecting oppressions are organized. Regardless of the particular intersections involved, structural disciplinary, hegemonic, and interpersonal domains of power reappear across quite different forms of oppression.[8]

I have been engaged in blending intersectionality with SRI with full awareness of critiques from feminist scholars such as Schüssler Fiorenza that SRI appears to promote scientific method by ignoring embodied epistemologies, being more concerned with technical aspects of the text than with critical injustices of context as a starting point. In fact, Schüssler Fiorenza has argued that SRI constitutes a "half-turn" in biblical studies, because it fails to acknowledge the contributions of feminist scholars to rhetorical criticism within the field.[9] She argued that this neglect stems from the unwillingness of those wanting to claim a "new turn" in rhetorical criticism to acknowledge the link between rhetoric and ethic. Joseph A. Marchal, drawing on Schüssler Fiorenza's analysis, also levels criticism at SRI for lumping together all feminist criticism under "ideological texture, as if feminist modes of analysis should not have an impact on literary, socio-cultural or theological interpretation."[10] Marchal's critique inspires my proposal for an *intersectional texture*, since ideological texture as traditionally presented in SRI seems to capture only a positionality and not a politics.

While taking the critiques of feminist scholars seriously, especially the role of ethics in rhetorical interpretation, I wish to argue that it is precisely because of my commitment to ethical modes of reading that I have proposed to explore the intersections of gender critical theory with the biblical interpretive analytic, SRI. It is exactly through "conceptual blending," to borrow an SRI category, of SRI analytical strategies and gender-critical perspective that advances can be made to conversations in the field.[11] As a heuristic analytics, SRI fittingly moves toward intersectionality, rather than in any way being opposed to it or in conflict with it. SRI draws on both the socio- (social context) and rhetorical (textual devices) as tools for examining texts, but much of the actual work focuses on the

---

[8] Patricia Hill Collins, "Gender, Black Feminism, and Black Political Economy," *Annals of the American Academy of Political and Social Science* 568 (2000): 18, quoted in Romero, *Introducing Intersectionality*, 51.

[9] Schüssler Fiorenza, "Challenging the Rhetorical Half-Turn," 29.

[10] Joseph A. Marchal, *Hierarchy, Unity and Imitation: A Feminist Rhetorical Analysis of Power Dynamics in Paul's Letter to the Philippians* (Atlanta: Society of Biblical Literature, 2006), 7.

[11] Vernon K. Robbins, "Conceptual Blending and Early Christian Imagination," in *Foundations for Sociorhetorical Exploration: A Rhetoric of Religious Antiquities Reader*, ed. Vernon K. Robbins, Robert H. von Thaden Jr., and Bart B. Bruehler, RRA 4 (Atlanta: SBL Press, 2016), 329–64.

inner, textual devices. Integrating the conceptual blending with gender-critical theory allows analysis to incorporate larger contexts into the interpretive environment. When the social is drawn in, it is often restricted to the social imaginary that surrounds the text—that is, the social and historical setting, more than social bodies—bodies that are gendered, raced, and classed. An intersectional gender-critical theory allows for the text to speak more vibrantly to context and for the context to more richly inform our understanding of the text.

Robbins suggests that the three areas of dialogue investigated by SRI are "the world created by the text, the world of the author and the world of the interpreter."[12] If one takes these three worlds seriously, then the critical theoretical optic in general and the gender-critical optic in particular seem obvious and even necessary. Here again, Robbins's claim is instructive. He suggests that SRI offers the option to move beyond historical studies, delving into the trajectory of cultural discourse, social contexts, and "rhetorical procedures of analysis which are more amenable to social and anthropological investigations."[13] This powerful claim, together with Robbins's original work on the various textures (inner texture, intertexture, social and cultural texture, ideological texture, and sacred texture) of the text as well as the later innovations on the analytical dimensions (rhetography, rhetology, and rhetorolect) led me to draw on this interpretive analytic extensively for my graduate studies.[14] The utility of this analytic for my interest in gender critical study seemed obvious for many reasons, not least of all because to study gender is to bring up for scrutiny the multiple ways in which power operates and functions to produce as well as destabilize norms in human relationships—norms in contemporary society that are often derived from sacred beliefs and texts.

Gaining mastery of SRI as a research analytic that pays attention to nuance and showcases the complexity of biblical texts was a good first step to whet my appetite around the textures of SRI, with a keen interest in investigating ideological texture and how it opens avenues for further scrutiny. My PhD dissertation blended gender critical theory with SRI to analyze the construction and representation of gender in the text of 1 Corinthians. Building upon previous work in my masters thesis, the PhD dissertation moved from a discussion of identity and gender theory to historical contextualization and finally to application. A leading contribution was elaboration, application, and development of SRI methodology

---

[12] Vernon K. Robbins, *Exploring the Texture of Texts: A Guide to Socio-rhetorical Interpretation* (Valley Forge, PA: Trinity Press International, 1996), 40.
[13] Vernon K. Robbins, *Jesus the Teacher: A Socio-rhetorical Interpretation of Mark* (Minneapolis: Fortress, 1992), 13.
[14] Robbins, *Exploring the Texture of Texts*; Robbins, *The Tapestry of Early Christian Discourse*; Robbins, "Conceptual Blending," 329–64, and Vernon K. Robbins, "Rhetography: A New Way of Seeing the Familiar Text," in Robbins, von Thaden, and Bruehler, *Foundations for Sociorhetorical Exploration*, 367–92.

by integrating SRI and gender-critical interpretive strategies to produce a novel deployment of SRI. Few SRI scholars have turned to gender-critical analysis. Here two distinctive fields of inquiry are brought into conversation with results that inform understanding of Paul's rhetoric in 1 Corinthians, but also for the study of New Testament texts more generally. Robert von Thaden offers a thoroughgoing SRI interpretation of portions of 1 Corinthians within a horizon of gender(ed) considerations.[15] This work is an important study on multiple levels, but its focus was limited to multiple textures and rhetorolects within SRI. My later work has combined key SRI elements such as rhetography, rhetorolect, intertexture, and ideological texture within a gender-critical framework that advances both SRI methodology and gender-critical assessment of the New Testament.[16]

Herein lies the distinctive contribution. Gender-critical theory is too often not brought into conversation with more traditional forms of historical-critical literary assessment. It is my contention that much can be gained by doing so and in this postulation lies the impetus for critical re-evaluation of SRI methodology. Particular textures of texts possess highly charged gendered images, thereby producing a type of gendered reasoning in biblical texts. Here the possibility for reconfigurations of existing SRI rhetography and rhetorolects or the development of new ones altogether are opened.

More recently Robbins, commenting on advances brought to SRI by the theories of critical spatiality and conceptual blending and their significance for rhetorolects, has noted "an awareness of the rhetography characteristic of each rhetorolect and the relation of that rhetography to its argumentative texture."[17] Robbins does not, however, directly indicate that rhetology and rhetography in early Christian writings also imply a highly gendered and complex intersectionality that blends together rhetology and rhetography and relies on gendered discourses taken from the hegemonic sex and gender systems of the ancient Mediterranean to construct its argumentation.[18] In this instance, SRI might need new terminology to describe the vivid depiction of rhetography that is gendered and create embodied and engendered "modes of understanding and belief" that

---

[15] Robert von Thaden Jr., *Sex, Christ, and Embodied Cognition: Paul's Wisdom for Corinth*, ESEC 16 (Atlanta: SBL Press, 2017); cf. von Thaden, "A Cognitive Turn: Conceptual Blending within a Sociorhetorical Framework," in Robbins, von Thaden, and Bruehler, *Foundations for Sociorhetorical Exploration*, 285–328.

[16] Johnathan Jodamus, "Gendered Ideology and Power in 1 Corinthians," *JECH* 6.1 (2016): 1–30; Jodamus, "Paul, the 'Real' Man: Constructions and Representations of Masculinity in 1 Corinthians," *Journal of Gender and Religion in Africa* 23 (2017): 68–94.

[17] Robbins, "Rhetography," 388.

[18] Robbins, "Rhetography," 367–92.

move toward new understandings of early Christian writings.[19] The traditional symbolic forms are highly gendered representations and serve to construct gendered identities and normativities. In this regard, gender is a tool to extrapolate key nuances of rhetography, rhetology, and ideology. Intersectionality theory can be a helpful analytic tool to demonstrate the complexities of power mechanisms and their impact on different people. For this reason, I think that intersectionality theory opens key caveats for SRI research and scholarship. At a minimum, the consequence of my argument is that SRI itself needs to reassess the gendered nature of the discourses used in its analysis. Moreover, it is evident that, as a result of this type of argument, SRI interpreters will need to reassess the degree their own methods reiterate the patterns of gendered power found in the New Testament texts under study.

Toward *Intersectional Texture*

As a heuristic interpretive analytics, SRI takes into consideration the embodied entanglement of texts and its tapestries to engage the complexity of New Testament texts. In this recognition lies the possibility for an expanded use of SRI in contemporary biblical studies by integrating *intersectional texture* within it. One of my PhD examiners suggested that the dissertation held great potential for a consideration of how intersectionality can be useful for an SRI analytic. When Kimberlé W. Crenshaw first coined the term "intersectionality" within the context of critical legal studies, she used the theory for specific interrogation of the plight and exclusion of black women whose "identity fixedness" as simultaneously black and women disqualified them from legal remedies.[20] Since then this expression has been adapted and may also be viewed as a critical analytical tool or a "thinking technology."[21] Implemented in this manner, intersectionality subverts binary notions of domination and focuses on the multiplicity and interdependence of social factors that participate in creating and sustaining power relations that function as discourses in the making of normativities, identities, and social relations.[22] At this stage intersectionality theory also becomes pivotal as a key theoretical framework that identifies types of bodies and *bodiliness* that

---

[19] Vernon K. Robbins, *The Invention of Christian Discourse*, RRA 1 (Dorset, UK: Deo, 2009), 6.
[20] Kimberlé W. Crenshaw, "Demarginalising the Intersection of Race and Sex."
[21] Nina Lykke, "Intersectional Analysis: Black Box or Useful Critical Feminist Thinking Technology?," in Lutz, Vivar, and Supik, *Framing Intersectionality*, 207–20; cf. "Using Intersectionality as an Analytic Tool," in *Intersectionality*, ed. Patricia Hill Collins and Sirma Bilge (Malden, MA: Polity Press, 2016), 2–5.
[22] Nira Yuval-Davis, "Beyond the Recognition and Re-distribution Dichotomy: Intersectionality and Stratification," in Lutz, Vivar, and Supik, *Framing Intersectionality*, 159, n. 2; Kimberlé W. Crenshaw, "Postcript," in Lutz, Vivar, and Supik, *Framing Intersectionality*, 221–33.

are constructed and cultivated in contemporary society. Bodies adhere to biblical texts as regulatory mechanisms that shape lived reality and experience. This is true particularly when such sacred texts are interpreted literally, and/or for moral and ethical purposes, or as a standard to gauge an individual or group's spirituality and value system and may become oppressive. Feminist scholars like Dube have lamented the life denying interpretations of such texts and have proposed innovative methods such as postcolonial feminist interpretation that offer more life affirming possibilities.[23]

Four years after my PhD, it seems to me that intersectionality is a well-suited bridge between what Schüssler Fiorenza puts forward as fundamentally different theoretical frameworks—Robbins's "relationism" and her framing of "kyriarchal domination."[24] This relationism can be found in Robbins's own insistence that the fundamental basis of SRI requires interpreters to create conscious plans of reading and rereading texts from different angles, with consideration given to different phenomena implicit in the texts.[25] This kind of interpretive approach is what Robbins and others have called an "interpretive analytics."[26] Robbins distinguishes SRI as an interpretive analytics in order to avoid confusing it with a particular research method. He mentions that a method employs a fixed number of analytical strategies with the intention of attaining a conclusion that is better than those employed by other methods. The objective of a method is to rule out the analytical strategies used by alternative methods by adopting better strategies to achieve a limited research objective. An interpretive analytics may be distinguished from a method because an analytics invites other analytical approaches to "illumine something the first set of strategies did not find, exhibit, discuss, and interpret."[27]

Schüssler Fiorenza argues that an ethic and rhetoric of enquiry "is necessary for overcoming the false dichotomy between engaged, socially located scholarship (e.g., feminist, postcolonial, African-American, queer, and other sub-

---

[23] Musa W. Dube, *Postcolonial Feminist Interpretation of the Bible* (Saint Louis: Chalice, 2000); Dube, "Rahab Says Hello to Judith: A Decolonizing Feminist Reading," in *Toward a New Heaven and a New Earth: Essays in Honor of Elisabeth Schüssler Fiorenza*, ed. Fernando F. Segovia (Maryknoll: Orbis, 2003), 54–72.

[24] Elisabeth Schüssler Fiorenza, "Disciplinary Matters: A Critical Rhetoric and Ethic of Inquiry," in *Rhetoric, Ethic, and Moral Persuasion in Biblical Discourse: Essays from the 2002 Heidelberg Conference*, ed. Thomas H. Olbricht and Anders Eriksson, ESEC 11 (New York: T&T Clark), 26.

[25] Robbins, *Exploring the Texture of Texts*, 40–41; cf. the discussion of "relationality" in Collins and Bilge, *Intersectionality*, 27–28, 48–62, 194–97.

[26] Robbins, *Exploring the Texture of Texts*, 12; Robbins, "Beginnings and Developments in Socio-rhetorical Interpretation," Emory University, 2004, http://tinyurl.com/SBL7103h; Robbins, *The Invention of Christian Discourse*, xiv, xvii.

[27] Robbins, *The Invention of Christian Discourse*, 5.

disciplines) and value-neutral 'scientific' (malestream) biblical interpretation."[28] The issue, therefore, is not that SRI closes off possibilities for multiple interpretations—it is that by opening up possibilities for multiple interpretations it can fall into the trap of *value-neutrality* where anything goes. This can be seen in the response by Robbins to Schüssler Fiorenza, which uses the metaphor of dance to suggest that we hold in tension our various methodological and theoretical positions as so-called equals:

> Moving forward, spiralling, stepping in place, turning around, and changing venue, we explore with each other, debate with one another, and disagree with each other as equals, inviting other voices into the dialogue in a manner that makes a rhetorical full-turn through scientific, humanist, malestream, feminist, ethnic, geographical, racial, economic, and social arenas of disputation, dialogue, and commentary.[29]

And yet we know, at least from the absence of black bodies at the rhetoric conferences in South Africa mentioned earlier, and the continued absence of black bodies in the guild of biblical scholars in South Africa, that not only are we not equals, but we are sometimes not invited to the dance at all. Ironically, while SRI scholars make reference to these operations of power in the text, it seems that the operations of power in context, particularly as they manifest in which bodies are present or absent on the rhetorical dance floor, are not seen as important considerations.[30] This is where my proposal of an *intersectional texture* that takes seriously the nexus of gender, race, class, and politics as embodied epistemology rather than merely as textual rhetoric is important. The glimmers of alignment with Robbins's earlier arguments are therefore taken to their logical conclusion in this proposal. According to Robbins, SRI offers a full turn in biblical interpretation and allows for "translocational, transtextual, trans-

---

[28] Schüssler Fiorenza, "Disciplinary Matters," 17.
[29] Vernon K. Robbins, "The Rhetorical Full-Turn in Biblical Interpretation: Reconfiguring Rhetorical-Political Analysis," in *Rhetorical Criticism and the Bible*, ed. Stanley E. Porter and Dennis L. Stamps, JSNTSup 195 (Sheffield: Sheffield Academic), 58–59.
[30] Cf. Charles A. Wanamaker, "By the Power of God: Rhetoric and Ideology in 2 Corinthians 10–13," in *Fabrics of Discourse: Essays in Honor of Vernon K. Robbins*, ed. David B. Gowler, L. Gregory Bloomquist, and Duane F. Watson (Harrisburg: Trinity Press International, 2003), 194–221; Wanamaker, "A Rhetoric of Power: Ideology and 1 Corinthians 1–4," in *Paul and the Corinthians: Studies on a Community in Conflict: Essays in Honour of Margaret Thrall*, ed. Trevor J. Burke and J. Keith Elliott, NovTSup 109 (Leiden: Brill, 2003), 115–37; Wanamaker, "The Power of the Absent Father: A Socio-rhetorical Analysis of 1 Corinthians 4:14–5:13," in *The New Testament Interpreted: Essays in Honour of Bernard C. Lategan*, ed. Cilliers Breytenbach, Johan C. Thom, and Jeremy Punt (Leiden: Brill, 2006), 339–64; Jodamus, "Gendered Ideology and Power in 1 Corinthians."

discursive, transcultural, and transtraditional interpretations that include disenfranchised voices, marginalized voices, recently liberated voices, and powerfully located voices."[31] Hence I believe that addition of an *intersectional texture* that provides a multidisciplinary, transdisciplinary, and dialogical interpretive framework for analyzing New Testament texts offers interpreters the possibility of a more holistic interpretation that is faithful to context.[32]

Drawing on Dreyfus and Rabinow,[33] Robbins asserts that:

> An interpretive analytics approaches texts as discourse and 'sees discourse as part of a larger field of power and practice whose relations are articulated in different ways by different paradigms.' The rigorous establishment of the relations of power and practice is the analytic dimension. The courageous writing of a story of the emergence of these relations is the interpretive dimension.[34]

In the courageous writing of my story as a black South African academic who often writes from the periphery of the guild, I am attempting to appeal for an ethical accountability for our reading strategies not to be mere rhetoric, but to take seriously our social locations. By adding an *intersectional texture* to the array of textures proposed by SRI practitioners the claim by Robbins, that "socio-rhetorical criticism is an approach to literature that focuses on values, convictions, and beliefs both in the texts we read and in the world in which we live"[35] takes on greater significance.

Contrary to what some feminist scholars have argued, this *intersectional texture* that takes the context of readers and their political commitments seriously aligns well with SRI analytic. SRI's multifaceted approach takes seriously the complexity of written documents as social and cultural constructions that serve as persuasive communications. The often employed historical-critical method, although valuable as a research tool, was "not

---

[31] Robbins, "The Rhetorical Full-Turn in Biblical Interpretation and Its Relevance for Feminist Hermeneutics," 123.

[32] Cf. Robbins *The Tapestry of Early Christian Discourse*, 16; *Exploring the Texture of Texts*, 2. Penner and Vander Stichele ("Unveiling Paul," 217) have noted that texts comprise "complex negotiations" and maintain that SRI offers a thickly textured and multifaceted approach to engage these intricacies within texts.Robbins, *Exploring the Texture of Texts*, 41; Robbins, *Jesus the Teacher*, xxv; Robbins, "The Rhetorical Full-Turn in Biblical Interpretation," 58.

[33] Hubert L. Dreyfus and Paul Rabinow, *Michel Foucault: Beyond Structuralism and Hermeneutics* (Chicago: University of Chicago Press, 1983), 199.

[34] Robbins, *The Tapestry of Early Christian Discourse*, 12; cf. Robbins, *The Invention of Christian Discourse*, xvii, xxiii.

[35] Robbins, *Exploring the Texture of Texts*, 1.

designed to explore the inner nature of texts as written discourse."[36] As Robbins asserts, "their role was, and still is, to answer a comprehensive range of historical and theological questions about people who can be identified as Christians and about events, institutions and beliefs that exhibit the history of the growth and expansion of the phenomenon we call Christianity."[37] One might go further and say that historical criticism was always interested in constructing the events and history behind the text. For this reason the text tended to be treated merely as a source of information rather than an object for investigation in its own right.

For example, and stemming from my own PhD research on 1 Corinthians, because Paul's identity itself has been formed by the engendered discursive patterns of ancient Mediterranean sex and gender systems, the gendered rhetoric of his argumentation cannot be divorced from the discursively formed gendered patterns of its context. There is then no unique subject with his own philosophical ideas addressing a situation, but someone who cannot but use what was strategically available to him even when there is a tinge of subversion in his rhetoric. Equally so, my body as an interpreter is produced by the marginal status I occupy as a black academic in the biblical guild in South Africa, as well as the complexity of my privileged position as a cis-gendered heterosexual male.

I maintain, on the basis of the above discussion, that SRI is well suited to assist with intersectional considerations. This is possible because SRI does not have to be used in a specific way, as Robbins has indicated.[38] Because SRI allows for the interaction of diverse investigative approaches, it also is suited for exploring diverse and complex forms of oppression and privilege. An intersectional approach takes seriously the argumentative nature of rhetoric and focuses on issues such as gender construction and identity within a text.[39]

---

[36] Robbins, *The Tapestry of Early Christian Discourse*, 8; See Fernando F. Segovia, "Liberation Hermeneutics: Revisiting the Foundations in Latin America," in *Toward a New Heaven and a New Earth: Essays in Honor of Elisabeth Schüssler Fiorenza*, ed. Fernando F. Segovia (Maryknoll: Orbis, 2003), 107–10, for a discussion that briefly traces the disciplinary history of historical criticism. Cf. Hanna Stenström, "Historical-Critical Approaches and the Emancipation of Women: Unfulfilled Promises and Remaining Possibilities," in Stichele and Penner, *Her Master's Tools?*, 31–46; Vander Stichele and Penner, "Mastering the Tools or Retooling the Masters? The Legacy of Historical-Critical Discourse," in Stichele and Penner, *Her Masters Tools?*, 1–30.

[37] Robbins, *The Tapestry of Early Christian Discourse*, 8.

[38] Robbins, *Exploring the Texture of Texts*, 5–6.

[39] Jorunn Økland, *Women in Their Place: Paul and the Corinthian Discourse of Gender and Sanctuary Space*, JSNTSup (London: T&T Clark, 2004); Todd Penner and Caroline Vander Stichele, "Unveiling Paul: Gendering Ethos in 1 Corinthians 11:2–16," in *Rhetoric, Ethic, and Moral Persuasion in Biblical Discourse: Essays from the 2002 Heidelberg Conference*, ed. Thomas H. Olbricht and Anders Eriksson, ESEC 11 (London: T&T Clark, 2005), 214–37.

Conclusion

The debates mentioned at the beginning of this paper raise important questions for SRI practitioners, perhaps even of an ethical kind, and have implications for framing SRI itself. This preliminary engagement serves to advance conversations on SRI and intersectional interpretive work on the New Testament and opens the opportunity to refine and perhaps even reform key aspects of SRI itself. It has been a great honor and privilege for me to share in discussion and to narrate my experience of using sociorhetorical interpretation in my own context and embodied epistemology. To echo where this paper started, "I wonder what people might say in 2050?" That, of course, will be thirty years after 2020, the year of the appearance of *Welcoming the Nations: International Sociorhetorical Explorations.*

An Exploration of Economic Rhetoric in the New Testament in Light of New Institutional Economics

Alex Hon Ho Ip

Introduction

24601 is not merely a number, but was Jean Valjean's prisoner number in Victor Hugo's famous novel *Les Misérables*. The use of the number to identify Valjean is indeed rhetoric addressing the economic situation in France during the years following the French Revolution, during the changes brought about by the Industrial Revolution, and in the social turmoil of the time. Jean Valjean was reduced to being a number. The ability to read the rhetoric behind the number depends on an understanding of the economic situation and the text.[1] There is a similar difficulty in reading the economic rhetoric in the New Testament, namely an understanding of the economic situation and its relationship to the text. Unfortunately, this is not a simple issue because there are methodological problems to be clarified before it becomes possible to investigate the details of the economic perspective of the text. Although the relevance of applying economics to the New Testament is accepted, scholars lack an analytical tool for applying economic findings to the process of New Testament interpretation systematically. Scholars have tried to incorporate relevant but fragmented economic information without clear methodological specification—either contextual economic status or economic issues—into the interpretative process, which sometimes creates more problems than clarifications.[2]

---

[1] The number was very personal for Victor Hugo as it stood for the date he believed he was conceived, 24 June 1801.

[2] There are a number of books that focus on economics and the New Testament, for example, Thomas R. Blanton IV and Raymond Pickett, eds., *Paul and Economics: A Handbook* (Minneapolis: Fortress, 2017); Richard Horsley, *Covenant Economics: A Biblical Vision of Justice for All* (Louisville: Westminster John Knox, 2009). Although they

My Economic Location and the Relevance of SRI

This section aims to introduce the thought and incentive for incorporating economic texture into New Testament interpretation. Economics has been considered irrelevant for analysis of the New Testament context since economics is modern theory interested in areas that simply did not exist in the market economy of antiquity. Living in Hong Kong, the world's most capitalist economy for more than forty years and being trained as an economist for more than ten years, I witnessed how deeply our lives and values are shaped by our economy. I used to believe that the rules of a capitalist society were fair because the market is free. Not until I personally encountered many poor families and witnessed their stories did I realize that the formal rules of the economy were supported and sustained by many values and informal institutions that are not true or fair. I started to realize that the economy is not merely a mechanism for allocation of resources; it shapes our values as well as our perceptions in many different ways. It is not only composed of formal rules but also informal institutions, and people may overlook its impact on their values, relationships, and perceptions. This view of the economy, that is, seeing economy as a set of institutions, comes from New Institutional Economics, and it helps us see the relevance of economics in interpretation of the New Testament.

Using Hong Kong as an example, we are one of the richest economies in the world in terms of per-capita government reserve and per-capita Gross Domestic Product, but our Gini-coefficient is the highest among the developed economies.[3] We have 1.38 million out of eight million people living below the poverty line as set by the government.[4] According to the fifteenth Annual Demographia International Housing Affordability Survey, the housing price in Hong Kong has

---

try to incorporate economics in their analyses, they do not specify clearly which economic theories they employ. Fragmentation or shifting among economic theories creates difficulties for discussing economic perspectives in the New Testament.

[3] Gini-coefficient is an economic indicator reflecting the income distribution between poor and wealthy. The value falls between 0 to 1, with 0 representing perfect equality and 1 representing perfect inequality. In June 2017, for Hong Kong it was 0.539, for the United States 0.411 and Singapore 0.4579. See Michelle Wong, "Why the Wealth Gap? Hong Kong's Disparity between Rich and Poor is Greatest in Forty-Five Years, So What Can be Done?," *South China Morning Post*, 27 September 2018, https://www.scmp.com/news/hong-kong/society/article/2165872/why-wealth-gap-hong-kongs-disparity-between-rich-and-poor.

[4] Announced by the Census and Statistics Department of Hong Kong Government, the poverty rate is 20.1 percent with 1.38 million people considered as poor. "Poverty Situation," Census and Statistics Department, The Government of the Hong Kong Special Administrative Region, https://tinyurl.com/SBL3814e.

been regarded as the "least affordable" in the world for the last eight years.[5] Ironically, Hong Kong has been selected by Fraser Institute as the freest economy in the world for twenty-four consecutive years, based on a set of criteria designed by the Institute.[6] It should not be difficult to see the relationship between the formal rules of a *freest* economy and its outcome of allocation of resources, that is, the discriminatory nature of capitalism. However, an even more provocative fact is that this outcome is rationalized and considered normal in Hong Kong. Furthermore, these indicators demonstrate a profound problem beyond the apparent issue of poverty: how can such institutions be sustained? What values are associated with the formal system and how can these values be implanted into society? The rationalization is done through planting in society the values that help justify capitalism through the informal institutions in society. For example, people in Hong Kong, including poor people themselves, generally believe that the free market is free, and, therefore, the outcome of competition obtained from the free market is just. More importantly, people have started to take this diversity between the poor and the rich for granted.

What I experienced in Hong Kong is not only the apparent problem of poverty but the relationship between the formal rules of the economy and the informal rules of the supporting values and attitudes embedded in our daily routine. For example, how can one justify and implant the value of competition? One means is through the education system. The value of competition is embedded in the education system. It is a well-known fact that the education system is highly competitive in Hong Kong. Schools are categorized into three different levels. Children have to compete for a *good* kindergarten to get into a *good* primary and secondary school. The outcome is that students spend more than fifty-five hours studying each week, which is higher than the standard forty-four hours per week set by the Organization for Economic Co-operation and Development and many European countries. Furthermore, our youth suicide rate is increasing alarmingly. Having to participate in such competition, people are trained, though unintentionally, to believe that the outcome of resources allocation is a result of the *free* competition but not the unfair rules of the game.

The above section does not aim to prove that Hong Kong is the way I have described it, but to introduce my investigation into the relationship between economic institutions and the New Testament. New Testament writers may not have been interested in *economic* matters in the narrow sense, but such a focus may address problems concerning values that may be in conflict with their values in

---

[5] "Fifteenth Annual Demographia International Housing Affordability Survey: 2019," Demographia, 21 January 2019, http://demographia.com/media_rls_2019.pdf.
[6] "Hong Kong Ranked World's Freest Economy for Twenty-Four Consecutive Years," The Government of the Hong Kong Special Administrative Region, https://www.info.gov.hk/gia/general/201802/02/P2018020200484.htm.

Christ. My location, both geographical and social in Hong Kong, provides me with the incentive to investigate the institutional aspect of an economy, both contemporary and first century Roman, and to explore how we could bring the institutional aspect of the Roman economy into interpretation of the New Testament. In light of this concern and motive, I found the interpretive analytic of sociorhetorical interpretation (SRI) to be a perfect platform to help me bring my concern in economics into New Testament interpretation. The most important reason is that SRI provides a systematic but not closed way to investigate a text. It maintains essential and relevant critical ways to investigate a text and allows new textures to be introduced with sufficient justification. As economics is not the major concern of New Testament scholars, we may not be able to read an economic agenda on the surface. However, as I mentioned above, economic institutions affect our lives and values on different levels, and we can read the impact of economics on the text through systematic ways and concepts suggested by SRI.

In light of my social, cultural, and economic location described above, this paper aims to explain how and to what extent SRI helps with showing the relevance of economics to New Testament interpretation. There are two inherent concerns underlying this agenda. First and foremost is the task of clarifying the focus and interests of economics as a field of study and theory. If there is no clarification of the perspective of economics discussed above, there will be unnecessary confusion. The word *economics* is often employed in its adjectival form, as, for example, in terms like *economic context*, *economic location*, and *economic parameter*, without defining exactly what is being considered. Scholars have assumed that there is a unique understanding of the meaning and content of *economic*. This produces confusion because there are different branches of economics and differing assumptions and methods. All of this affects how texts are interpreted. I will clarify this in the next section and argue that New Institutional Economics provides relevant tools for investigating the Roman economy during the time of the New Testament.

The second concern is how economics relates to the New Testament and how its relevance can be understood. While scholars may agree that ancient Mediterranean economics is an important aspect of New Testament interpretation, there is a lack of relevant and consistent tools that can bring it to bear on the text. In this regard, I will argue in the third section of this paper that sociorhetorical analytics such as rhetorolects and rhetography provide excellent platforms and tools for incorporating economic analysis and interpretation into investigation of the New Testament. The flow of this paper runs in the following way: after introducing the nature of New Institutional Economics (NIE) and explaining how it provides a new view for understanding the Roman economy, I will suggest two specific ways in which SRI helps integrate the contributions from economic analysis into New Testament interpretation.

The Nature of NIE and How It Helps Us Understand the Roman Economy

Before introducing the nature of NIE and explaining why it provides a useful economic perspective for New Testament interpretation, I will describe a bit of the methodological controversy. There has been an ongoing debate about whether economic theory can be used to analyze ancient economies. This debate has its roots in presuppositions concerning the market and other social norms and values. This diversity of understanding also hinders biblical scholars from bringing economics into New Testament interpretation. In order to appreciate this debate, I will introduce three key figures and their main thoughts. Karl Polanyi introduced the concept of *embedded economy* to suggest the dominance of social values and norms over market mechanism.[7] He rightly pointed out that the market is not necessarily the major form or institution to facilitate the running of the economy. However, he wrongly infers that "any economy, as a rule, is submerged in its social relationships."[8] Michael Rostovtzeff, on the other side of the camp, suggests that the Roman economy was grand enough to allow for use of modern market driven economic theory for investigation.[9] Moses Finley does not agree with Rostovtzeff and suggests that we lack relevant and sufficient data to justify the use of modern economic theory to analyze ancient economies. Additionally, starting from the analysis of the etymology of *oikonomia*, he suggests that there are other social values and hierarchies affecting the allocation of resources, which accounts for the absence of the independent concept of economy in Roman society.[10] This debate cannot be answered by either neoclassical or neoliberal economic theories that depend heavily on the assumption of the existence of market.

In recent decades, Douglass North has developed a framework for applying NIE to economic history, which helps bridge the gap. North suggests that institutions should be the focus of analysis instead of markets, and markets are only one form of institution. North defines institution as "a set of constraints on behavior in the form of rules and regulations; a set of procedures to detect deviations from the rules and regulations; and, finally, a set of moral, ethical behavioral norms which define the contours that constrain the way in which the

---

[7] Karl Polanyi, *Great Transformation: The Political and Economic Origins of Our Time* (Boston: Beacon, 2001).
[8] Polanyi, *Great Transformation*, 48.
[9] Michael Rostovtzeff, *The Social and Economic History of the Roman Empire* (Oxford: Clarendon, 1988), 18–21.
[10] Moses Finley, *The Ancient Economy* (Berkeley: University of California Press, 1999), 33–34.

rules and regulations are specified and enforcement is carried out."[11] The value of North's focus on institutions is its applicability to a non-market dominant Roman economy. Additionally, based on North's approach, analysis does not rely on numerical data but focuses on much existing historical data, including Roman legal documents, government edicts, Roman literature, and a range of information gathered from excavation sites that tell us about the daily life of people living in the Roman Empire.

At the heart of this discussion is a presupposition that *institution* is the bridging concept between NIE and New Testament studies. An institution is different than an *organization*, because organization refers to players of the economy while institution refers to the rules of the game. Institutions are analogous to rules that facilitate and to some extent determine transactions or, broadly speaking, human interactions.[12] Institutions include both formal and informal rules. The basic belief of NIE is that players try to find an institution that helps them minimize their transaction cost and cost in facing uncertainty. Both formal and informal rules are embedded in daily lives that define human interactions.[13] The key focus of NIE is the relationship among informal institution, formal institution, and the final economic outcome. Therefore, NIE sheds new light on how formal and informal institutions shape human relationships and other economic parameters that interest New Testament scholars. The new perspective developed from the NIE approach provides a new hermeneutical lens for the context. For example, we might view Roman law simply as law without noticing that it also serves an economic purpose and is part of the formal institution or rules that shape human interactions. Therefore, to understand a New Testament situation from an NIE perspective requires specifically looking at how different institutions work together to serve economic purposes. It is in this sense that NIE is relevant to New Testament studies, since NIE provides a new analytical tool for us to understand the historical data from an economic perspective.

With the help of NIE, we can have a more systematic and coherent view of the Roman economy. The underlying values, the legal and formal system, daily practices, and subsequent economic outcomes are all correlated. By investigating both formal and informal institutions, we can have a coherent picture of the values, system, and outcome from an economic perspective. For example, under NIE, the economic perspective of Roman slavery is no longer merely about considering the practice or system for management of slaves, but also how Roman values and beliefs justify the system, the economic function of the legal institu-

---

[11] Douglass North, "Transaction Cost, Institutions and Economic History," *Journal of Institutional and Theoretical Economics* 140 (1984): 8.

[12] John Groenewegen at al., *Institutional Economics: An Introduction* (London: Palgrave Macmillan, 2010), 24–25.

[13] Groenewegen at al., *Institutional Economics*, 26.

tions, and slaves' living conditions.[14] One more example is the Roman household, as household relationships are not merely familial but are economic relationships supported by both formal and informal institutions. Therefore, regardless of metaphorical language or verses directly addressing household relationships, we can have deeper insight for understanding the nuances of the relationships. What is lacking now? It is the textual analytical framework that can embrace this new contextual information in the text.

The Contributions of SRI for Incorporating Economics into Analysis

SRI contributes to incorporating economics to New Testament analysis in two ways. First, since economics is not a single thing but a set of factors, the investigation of the impact of economic factors on the text requires a concept that can embrace this interweaving nature of economics. The concept of textural analysis of a text provides both the right interpretive lens as well as the platform for the investigation. Economics is neither the objective nor the theological argument of New Testament writers. However, economics does act as an important texture that constitutes an important feature of the meaning of many texts. It is crucial to analyze the possible ways economic institutions exert influences on their audiences through the text. This is a second contribution of SRI in that it brings new and cutting edge research to rhetorical analysis, which helps us hear more clearly the inner rhetorical voices in the text.

Economic Texture

Since economics influences a text not just through one layer of a society but a set of corporate factors, the cooperation of both formal and informal institutions is required. To say that economics is a set of corporate factors implies that different institutions are not independent factors, but are interrelated to serve economic purposes.[15] The SRI concept of interwoven textures fits well with this nature of economics. Economic texture embraces both sociocultural and ideological textures, since the economic system constitutes the believing system and formal institutions that influence people's lives and relationships. In light of this, if we begin with a text that may contain an economic element, to examine the economic layer of the text we need to examine not only one factor but a set of corporate factors that may include the believing system—what we sometimes

---

[14] Alex Hon Ho Ip, *A Socio-rhetorical Interpretation of the Letter to Philemon in Light of the New Institutional Economics: An Exhortation to Transform a Master-Slave Economic Relationship into a Brotherly Loving Relationship* WUNT 2/444 (Tübingen: Mohr Siebeck, 2017), 120.
[15] Ip, *Socio-rhetorical Interpretation*, 113–14.

call the institutional environment in NIE—as well as formal and informal institutions.[16]

Analysis of economic texture can be performed like the analysis of other textures, but with a specific focus on the impact of how economic factors, based on NIE analysis, affect the layers of the text. In this way, it is possible to understand the economic impact of a text. The exact meaning of the economic texture, however, depends on findings from both inner texture and intertexture. The inner texture and intertexture may help to define what problem is addressed in the economic texture. This is important as it avoids the problem of mirror reading of the text.[17] For example, when considering the economic context of poverty, we should examine not only the outcome of poverty, but the system creating it and the value system behind it, since the text may address not only the outcome but also the system itself or the believing system sustaining it. Using economic texture as an additional framework within sociorhetorical interpretation makes it easier to analyze the corporate nature of economic factors.

Rhetoric, Rhetorolects, and Rhetography

The contribution of rhetoric, rhetorolects, and rhetography provides a legitimate sphere for analyzing how New Testament writers address various layers of economic issues. An economic matter is not simply a logical or ethical issue that an author can use logos to argue for or against. It can be a deeper issue that audiences not only practice but also believe to be morally correct. So how could a New Testament writer address issues created by different institutions? How could one address the values of audiences that not only believe institutions to be right but practice them every day? If we take this into consideration, it becomes evident that Paul's main problem in the letter to Philemon is not simply to tell Philemon what is right, but to exert the greatest rhetorical power possible to lead Philemon to *see* the problem of the existing economic relationship and the need, based on Paul's theological thoughts, to transform this relationship.

With the help of economic texture, we may more clearly understand various things the text addresses related to economics. It is not easy to see the relevance of the text to economic texture, however, since there is not much explicit *economic vocabulary* in the New Testament even when the text implicitly addresses economic matters. Scholars may overlook the text's economic relevance or use their own basic understandings of economics to assume that only explicit economic concepts are significant (such as money, trade, wealth, or poverty). The result will be that the analysis related to economics seems insignificant and mar-

---

[16] Ip, *Socio-rhetorical Interpretation*, 113–16.
[17] John Barclay, "Mirror-Reading a Polemical Letter: Galatians as a Test Case," *JSNT* 31 (1987): 73–74.

ginal to mainstream New Testament studies. However, the broader and deeper perspective and rich analysis of Greek and Roman rhetoric provides many concrete options for interpreting the economic texture in the text. For example, the concept of metaphor reminds us that figurative language may lead audiences to *see* what they cannot see in their economic context.[18] Different kinds of formal rhetoric help us to see the intention of the author beyond the surface meaning of a text into its structure. More importantly, related to economics, these rhetorical concepts allow us to see ways the text addresses different layers of economic issues. This extension of the text's possible meaning provides a new and legitimate ground to interpret possible economic references in the text.

Economics does not create a new form of rhetoric, but a new need and new target for the rhetoric. In order to address economic issues, New Testament writers had to consider the nature of the problems they were addressing and generate specific ways to speak to various aspects of economic issues. In reading the rhetoric of the text in relation to economics, we can bring different layers of the economic texture into consideration and ask about the ways writers addressed them, which we might not notice without the awareness of rhetoric. Economics, according to NIE, affects people at least through three different layers. How did values and belief systems shape people's beliefs? How did formal institutions affect the attitudes and beliefs among people? How did formal and informal institutions shape relationships among people and create economic outcomes? With the help of the concepts of rhetoric and economic texture, we can investigate how writers addressed different levels of economic texture through concepts from rhetorical analysis such as deliberative rhetorical structure, ethos, pathos, logos, topos, and, sometimes, improvised forms of rhetoric.[19]

The contribution of rhetorolects and rhetography cannot be overlooked. Beginning with Kennedy's idea of the blending of radical and worldly rhetoric, Robbins suggests that at least six rhetorolects blend dynamically in early Christian discourse as a result of the rhetography in its rhetoric.[20] These concepts are very useful and supportive tools for understanding the economic relevance of a text. The most fundamental reason comes from the way economic activities influence people's lives. The impact of economics is not merely an intellectual notion that one can use logos to argue for or against, but is embedded in daily activities and deeply implanted in people through the daily operation of society.

---

[18] Lynn R Huber, "Knowing Is Seeing: Theories of Metaphor Ancient, Medieval, and Modern," in *Foundations for Sociorhetorical Exploration: A Rhetoric of Religious Antiquity*, ed. Vernon K. Robbins, Robert H. von Thaden, Jr., and Bart B. Bruehler, RRA 4 (Atlanta: SBL Press, 2016), 239–40.

[19] Ip, *A Socio-rhetorical Interpretation*, 54–55.

[20] Vernon K. Robbins, Robert H. von Thaden Jr., and Bart B. Bruehler, introduction to Robbins, von Thaden, and Bruehler, *Foundations for Sociorhetorical Exploration*, 5.

People are affected by different levels of economic institutions through the values of their peers and through rules of the society. Values condition our seeing or sometimes make us blind. Therefore, we need to bring a new vision in order to take up new values or relationships.

The importance of rhetorolects and rhetography comes from their contribution to our attention to rhetorical power in Christian discourse. The nature of the problem created by economics concerns not only arguments of right and wrong, but conflict between Christian values and worldly values. However, the worldly values were embedded in formal and informal institutions of the economy. These worldly values were not formally taught, but planted in people through their daily participation in the social *game* where rules were set according to these values. In this respect, addressing these values cannot be done only through logos or formal rhetoric, but by employing additional rhetorical skills that can generate significant rhetorical power for audiences.

To address these worldly economic values, New Testament writers had to invent language based on Christian beliefs. They still used some existing rhetorical forms such as deliberative rhetoric, but participated in invention as they addressed new conflicting values. Besides, as stated above, these values require more than argument or logos—that is, stronger means of persuasion. In light of this, there is a need to use stronger rhetorical influence upon audiences in order to exert influence to counter these values. This also explains the reason for pervasive rhetography in the New Testament as writers used metaphorical and figurative language to help audiences to see what they could not otherwise see because of their strongly implanted values.

Conclusion

Economics is an important aspect of New Testament discourse that has been overlooked by scholars for many years due to the methodological problem of finding an appropriate model for understanding the ancient economy. I hope this paper makes the case that NIE is an appropriate economic theory that helps scholars investigate the importance of economics for New Testament interpretation. With the help of NIE, SRI opens space for study of the economic texture of a text and for reading the rhetoric related to different layers of economics. In my view, NIE and SRI form a good partnership for reading the rhetoric of economics in the text.

Bibliography

Abraham, Christina. "The Devil Is in the Details: A Socio-cultural Reading of the Gerasene Narrative in Mark." MA thesis, Queen's University, Kingston, Ontario, 2016.

Afioga, Latu. "A *Tuagane* (Brother to a Sister) Reading of Jesus' Conversation with the Syro-phoenician Woman in Mark 7:24–30." BD thesis, Malua Theological College, Samoa, 2016.

Aiono, Fanaafi Le Tagaloa. *O Motugaafa*. Alafua, University of the South Pacific: Le Lamepa Press, 1996.

Antonyraj, Sebastian Victor. "The Centurion, A Transformational Leader: A Socio-rhetorical Analysis of Matthew 8.5–13." PhD diss., Pontifical University of Saint Thomas Aquinas, Rome, 2017.

Ao, Chubamongba. "'In All the Work of Your Hands' in Deuteronomy: An Inquiry on Rhetoric of Work." DTh diss., South Asia Theological Research Institute, Union Biblical Seminary, Pune, Maharashtra, India, 2017.

Australian Research Council Centre of Excellence for Coral Reef Studies, James Cook University, Townsville, Queensland, Australia. "Only Only 7% of the Great Barrier Reef has avoided coral bleaching." https://www.coralcoe.org.au/media-releases/only-7-of-the-great-barrier-reef-has-avoided-coral-bleaching.

Asumang, Annang. "The Presence of the Shepherd: A Rhetographic Exegesis of Psalm 23." *Conspectus: The Journal of the South African Theological Seminar* 9 (2010): 1–23.

Bailey, Jon Nelson. "Paul's Political Paraenesis in Romans 13:1–7." *Restoration Quarterly* 46 (2004): 11–28.

Barclay, John. "Mirror-Reading a Polemical Letter: Galatians as a Test Case." *JSNT* 31 (1987): 73–93.

Barton, Stephen. *Discipleship and Family Ties in Mark and Matthew*. SNTSMS 80. Cambridge: Cambridge University Press, 1994.

Beech, Timothy. "A Socio-rhetorical Analysis of the Development and Function of the Noah-Flood Narrative in *Sibylline Oracles* 1–2." PhD diss., Saint Paul University, Ottawa, 2007.

Berquist, Jon L. "Theories of Space and Construction of the Ancient World." Pages 151–76 in *Foundations for Sociorhetorical Exploration: A Rhetoric of Religious Antiquity*

Reader. Edited by Vernon K. Robbins, Robert H. von Thaden Jr., and Bart B. Bruehler. RRA 4. Atlanta: SBL Press, 2016.

Bertschmann, Helene Dorothea. "Bowing before Christ—Nodding to the State? Reading Paul Politically with Oliver O' Donovan and John Howard Yoder." PhD diss., Durham University, Durham, 2012.

Betz, Hans Dieter. *Galatians: A Commentary on Paul's Letter to the Churches in Galatia*. Hermeneia. Philadelphia; Fortress, 1979.

Beyrouti, François. "Discerning a 'Rhetorics of Catechesis' in Origen of Alexandria's *Commentary on the Gospel of John:* A Sociorhetorical Analysis of Book XIII:3–42 (John 4:13–15)." PhD diss., Saint Paul University, Ottawa, 2013.

Bhabha, Homi K. *The Location of Culture*. New York, NY: Routledge, 1994.

Blanton, Thomas R. IV, and Raymond Pickett, eds. *Paul and Economics: A Handbook*. Minneapolis: Fortress, 2017.

Bloomquist, L. Gregory. "A Contemporary Exegesis at the Edges of Chaos." *Religion & Theology* 11.1 (2004): 1–38.

———. "Eyes Wide Open, Seeing Nothing: The Challenge of the Gospel of John's Non-visualizable Texture for Readings Using Visual Texture." Pages 121–67 in *The Art of Visual Exegesis: Rhetoric, Texts, Images*. Edited by Vernon K. Robbins, Walter S. Melion, and Roy R. Jeal. ESEC 19. Atlanta: SBL Press, 2017.

———. "The Intertexture of Lukan Apocalyptic Discourse." Pages 45–68 in *The Intertexture of Apocalyptic Discourse in the New Testament*. Edited by Duane F. Watson. SymS 14. Atlanta: Society of Biblical Literature, 2002.

———. "Methodological Criteria for the Determination of Apocalyptic Rhetoric: A Suggestion for the Expanded Use of Socio-rhetorical Analysis." Pages 181–203 in *Vision and Persuasion: Rhetorical Dimensions of Early Jewish and Christian Apocalyptic Discourse*. Edited by Greg Carey and L. Gregory Bloomquist. Saint Louis: Chalice, 1999.

———. "Methodology for Rhetography and Visual Exegesis of the Gospel of John." Pages 89–120 in *The Art of Visual Exegesis: Rhetoric, Texts, Images*. Edited by Vernon K. Robbins, Walter S. Melion, and Roy R. Jeal. ESEC 19. Atlanta: SBL Press, 2017.

———. "Patristic Reception of a Lukan Healing Account: A Contribution to a Socio-rhetorical Response to Willi Braun's *Feasting and Social Rhetoric in Luke 14*, SNTSMS 85 (Cambridge: University Press, 1995)." Pages 105–34 in *Healing in Religion and Society, From Hippocrates to the Puritans*. Edited by S. Muir and J. K. Coyle. Studies in Religion and Society 43. Lewiston: Edwin Mellen Press, 1999.

———. "Paul's Inclusive Language: The Ideological Texture of Romans 1." Pages 165–93 in *Fabrics of Discourse: Essays in Honor of Vernon K. Robbins*. Edited by David B. Gowler, L. Gregory Bloomquist, and Duane F. Watson. New York: Trinity Press International, 2003. Repr., pages 119–48 in *Foundations for Socio-rhetorical Exploration: A Rhetoric of Religious Antiquity Reader*. Edited by Vernon K. Robbins, Robert H. von Thaden Jr., and Bart B. Bruehler. RRA 4. Atlanta: SBL Press, 2016.

———. "The Pesky Threads of Robbins's Rhetorical Tapestry: Vernon K. Robbins's Genealogy of Rhetorical Criticism." Pages 201–24 in *Genealogies of New Testament*

Rhetorical Criticism. Edited by Troy W. Martin. Minneapolis: Fortress, 2014.

———. "A Possible Direction for Providing Programmatic Correlation of Textures in Socio-rhetorical Analysis." Pages 61–96 in *Rhetorical Criticism and the Bible.* Edited by Stanley E. Porter and Dennis L. Stamps. JSNTSup 195. Sheffield: Sheffield Academic, 2002.

———. "Rhetoric, Culture, and Ideology: Socio-rhetorical Analysis in the Reading of New Test-ament Texts." Pages 115–46 in *Rhetorics in the New Millennium: Promise and Fulfillment.* Edited by James D. Hester and J. David Hester. SAC. New York: T&T Clark, 2010.

———. "The Rhetoric of Suffering in Paul's Letter to the Philippians: Socio-rhetorical Reflections and Further Thoughts on a Post-colonial Contribution to the discussion." *Theoforum* 35.2 (2004): 195–223.

———. "Rhetorical Argumentation and the Culture of Apocalyptic: A Socio-rhetorical Analysis of Luke 21." Pages 173–209 in *The Rhetorical Interpretation of Scripture: Essays from the 1996 Malibu Conference.* Edited by Stanley E. Porter and Dennis L. Stamps. JSNTSup 180. Sheffield: Sheffield Academic, 1999.

———. "The Role of Argumentation in the Miracle Stories of Luke-Acts: Towards a Fuller Identification of Miracle Discourse for Use in Socio-rhetorical Analysis." Pages 85–124 in *Miracle Discourse in the New Testament.* Edited by Duane F. Watson. Atlanta: Society of Biblical Literature, 2012.

———. "The Role of the Audience in the Determination of Argumentation: The Gospel of Luke and the Acts of the Apostles." Pages 157–73 in *Rhetorical Argumentation in Biblical Texts: Essays from the Lund 2000 Conference.* Edited by Anders Eriksson, Thomas H. Olbricht, and Walter Übelacker. ESEC 8. Harrisburg: Trinity Press International, 2002.

———. "Suffering and Joy: Subverted by Joy in Paul's Letter to the Philippians." *Interpretation* 61.3 (2007): 270–82.

———. "Visualizing Philippians: Ancient Rhetorical Practice Meets Cognitive Science through Sociorhetorical Interpretation." Pages 265–84 in *Paul and Ancient Rhetoric: Theory and Practice in the Hellenistic Context.* Edited by Stanley E. Porter and Bryan R. Dyer. Cambridge: Cambridge University Press, 2016.

Boer, Roland. "Resistance Versus Accommodation: What to Do with Romans 13?" Pages 109–22 in *Postcolonial Interventions: Essays in Honor of R. S. Sugirtharajah.* Edited by Tat-Siong Benny Liew. Sheffield: Sheffield Phoenix, 2009.

Bonneau, Normand. "Socio-rhetorical Interpretation's 'Narrational Texture' in Dialogue with Narratology." *Theoforum* 46 (2015), 43–52.

Botha, Jan. *Subject to Whose Authority? Multiple Readings of Romans 13.* ESEC 4. Atlanta: Scholars Press, 1994.

Boyer, Susan. "Exegesis of Romans 13: 1–7." *Brethren Life and Thought* 32 (1987): 208–16.

Braun, Willi. *Feasting and Social Rhetoric in Luke 14.* SNTSMS 85. Cambridge: Cambridge University Press, 1995.

———. "Social-rhetorical Interests: Context." Pages 93–95 in *Whose Historical Jesus?*

Edited by William E. Arnal. Studies in Christianity and Judaism 7. Waterloo: Wilfrid Laurier Press, 1997.

Bruehler, Bart B. "From the Place: A Theoretical Framework for the Social-Spatial Analysis of Luke." Pages 197–236 in *Foundations for Sociorhetorical Exploration: A Rhetoric of Religious Antiquity Reader*. RRA 4. Atlanta: SBL Press, 2016.

Camp, Claudia V. "Storied Space, or, Ben Sira 'Tells' a 'Temple.'" Pages 177–96 in *Foundations for Sociorhetorical Exploration: A Rhetoric of Religious Antiquity Reader*. RRA 4. Atlanta: SBL Press, 2016.

Canavan, Rosemary. *Clothing the Body of Christ at Colossae. A Visual Construction of Identity*. WUNT 2.334. Tübingen: Mohr Siebeck, 2012.

Carney, T. F. *The Shape of the Past: Models and Antiquity*. Lawrence, KS: Coronado Press, 1975.

Collins, Patricia Hill. *Black Feminist Thought: Knowledge, Empowerment and Consciousness*. New York: Routledge, 2000.

———. "Gender, Black Feminism, and Black Political Economy." *Annals of the American Academy of Political and Social Science* 568 (2000): 41–53.

Combrink, H. J. Bernard. "The Challenge of Making and Redrawing Boundaries: A Perspective on Socio-rhetorical Criticism." *Nederduitse Gereformeerde Teologiese Tydskrif* 40 (1999): 18–30.

———. "The Challenges and Opportunities of a Socio-rhetorical Commentary." *Scriptura* 79 (2002): 106–21.

———. "The Contribution of Socio-rhetorical Interpretation to the Reformed Interpretation of Scripture." Pages 91–106 in *Reformed Theology: Identity and Ecumenicity II: Biblical Interpretation in the Reformed Tradition*. Edited by Wallace M. Alston Jr. and Michael Welker. Grand Rapids: Eerdmans, 2007.

———. "The Rhetoric of the Church in the Transition from the Old to the New South Africa: Socio-rhetorical Criticism and Ecclesiastical Rhetoric." *Neot* 32 (1998), 289–307.

———. "Shame on the Hypocritical Leaders in the Church: A Socio-rhetorical Interpretation of the Reproaches in Matthew 23." Pages 1–35 in *Fabrics of Discourse: Essays in Honor of Vernon K. Robbins*. Edited by David B. Gowler, L. Gregory Bloomquist, and Duane F. Watson. Harrisburg, PA: Trinity Press International, 2003.

Corlett-MacDonald, Nina. "Jesus and 'Other' Deviants: A Narrative Labelling Study of 'Aloneness' in Mark 5:1–20." PhD diss., Flinders University, South Australia, 2016.

Crenshaw, Kimberlé W. "Mapping the Margins: Intersectionality, Identity Politics, and Violence against Women of Color." *Stanford Law Review* 46 (1991): 1241–99.

———. "Demarginalising the Intersection of Race and Sex: A Black Feminist Critique of Anti-discrimination Doctrine, Feminist Theory and Anti-racist Politics." *University of Chicago Legal Forum* 140 (1989): 139–67.

———. "Postscript." Pages 221–33 in *Framing Intersectionality: Debates on a Multi-Faceted Concept in Gender Studies*. Edited by Helma Lutz, Maria Teresa Herrera Vivar, and Linda Supik. Burlington VT; Farnham, Surrey, UK: Ashgate, 2011.

Czachesz, István. "Socio-rhetorical Exegesis of Acts 9:1–30." *Communio Viatorum* (Praha) 37 (1995): 5–32.

"Fifteenth Annual Demographia International Housing Affordability Survey: 2019." Demographia. http://demographia.com/media_rls_2019.pdf.

Draper, Jonathan A. "'Humble Submission to Almighty God' and Its Biblical Foundation: Contextual Exegesis of Romans 13: 1–7." *Journal of Theology for Southern Africa* 63 (1988): 30–38.

Dreyfus, Hubert L., and Paul Rabinow. *Michel Foucault: Beyond Structuralism and Hermeneutics.* Chicago: University of Chicago Press, 1983.

Dube, Musa W. *Postcolonial Feminist Interpretation of the Bible.* Saint Louis: Chalice, 2000.

———. "Rahab Says Hello to Judith: A Decolonizing Feminist Reading." Pages 54–72 in *Toward a New Heaven and a New Earth: Essays in Honor of Elisabeth Schüssler Fiorenza.* Edited by Fernando F. Segovia. Maryknoll: Orbis, 2003.

Dunn, James D. G. "Romans 13.1–7: A Charter for Political Quietism?" *Ex Auditu* 2 (1986): 55–68.

Dyck, Harold J. "The Christian and the Authorities in Romans 13: 1–7." *Direction* 14 (1985): 44–50.

Dyson, Michael Eric. *Reflecting Black: African-American Cultural Criticism.* Minneapolis: University of Minnesota, 1993.

Eilperin, Juliet. "Great Barrier Reef has lost half its coral since 1985 new study says." *The Washington Post,* 1 October 2012.

Fatilua, Fatilua. "The Church and Court Litigation: A Socio-rhetorical Analysis of 1 Corinthians 6:1–11." BD thesis, Malua Theological College, Samoa, 2016.

———. *Fāiā Analysis of Romans 13:1–17: Integrating A Samoan Perspective with Socio-rhetorical Criticism.* MTh thesis, Pacific Theological College, Suva, Fiji, 2018.

Fauconnier, Gilles, and Mark Turner. *The Way We Think: Conceptual Blending and the Mind's Hidden Complexities.* New York: Basic Books, 2002.

Feagaimaalii-Luamanu, Joyetter. "Samoa Head of State Approves Law to Tax Himself, Church Ministers." *Samoa Observer.* 3 July 2017.

Feinberg, Paul D. "The Christian and Civil Authorities." *Master's Seminary Journal* 10 (1999): 87–99.

Fernandez, Cyprian E. *Identity in Conflict: A Socio-rhetorical Reading of the Markan Story of Jesus.* Bengaluru, India: Asian Trading Corporation, 2016.

Finbow, Douglas. "The Wisdom of the Scribe: A Socio-rhetorical and Theological Interpretation of Sirach 38:24–39:11." PhD diss., Saint Paul University, 2017.

Finley, Moses. *The Ancient Economy.* Berkeley: University of California Press, 1999.

Fitzmyer, Joseph A. *Romans: A New Translation with Introduction and Commentary.* AB. New York: Doubleday, 1993.

Fung, Ben. "The Healing of the Blind Man in Bethsaida in Mark 8:22–26." PhD diss., Saint Paul University, in progress.

———. "Review of *Foundations for Sociorhetorical Exploration.*" *Theoforum* 47.2 (2016–2017): 500–502.

Gadamer, Hans-Georg. *Truth and Method.* Translated by Joel Weinsheimer and Donald G Marshall. New York: Seabury, 1975.

Gager, John G. *Kingdom and Community: The Social World of Early Christianity.* Englewood Cliffs NJ: Prentice Hall, 1975.

Geisterfer, Priscilla. "Full Turns and Half Turns: Engaging the Dialogue/Dance between Elisabeth Schüssler Fiorenza and Vernon Robbins." Pages 129–44 in *Her Master's Tools? Feminist and Postcolonial Engagements of Historical-Critical Discourse.* Edited by Caroline Vander Stichele and Todd Penner. GPBS 9. Atlanta: Society of Biblical Literature, 2005.

Gowler, David B. "The Development of Socio-rhetorical Criticism." Pages 1–36 in *New Boundaries in Old Territory: Form and Social Rhetoric in Mark.* Edited by Vernon K. Robbins and David B. Gowler. ESEC 3. New York: Lang, 1994.

———. "The End of the Beginning: The Continuing Maturation of Socio-rhetorical Analysis." Pages 1–45 in *Sea Voyages and Beyond: Emerging Strategies in Socio-rhetorical Interpretation.* Edited by Vernon K. Robbins. ESEC 14. Atlanta: SBL Press, 2010, 2018.

———. "Socio-rhetorical Interpretation: Textures of a Text and Its Reception." *JSNT* 33 (2010): 191–206.

Groenewegen, John, Antoon Spithoven, and Annette Van Den Berg. *Institutional Economics: An Introduction.* London: Palgrave Macmillan, 2010.

Gruca-Macaulay, Alexandra. *Lydia as a Rhetorical Construct in Acts: A Sociorhetorical and Theological Interpretation.* ESEC 18. Atlanta: SBL Press, 2016.

———. "A Socio-rhetorical Assessment of Conclusions from the History of Interpretation of the Role of Women in Luke-Acts." MA thesis, Saint Paul University, Ottawa, 2006.

Gunn, Éloi. "Fundamentalist Religious Discourse in Process of Radicalization to Violence—Analysis." *Canadian Military Journal.* 4 May 2018. https://tinyurl.com/SBL3814.

Gunn, Têtê Délali. "Prosopopée idéologique de Paul: Une lecture socio-rhétorique du discours de Paul à Athènes: Actes 17,15–18,1)." PhD diss., Saint Paul University, Ottawa, 2006.

Habel, Norman C., and Peter Trudinger, eds. *Exploring Ecological Hermeneutics.* SymS 46. Atlanta: Society of Biblical Literature, 2008.

Hammer, Keir. "Disambiguating Rebirth: A Socio-rhetorical Exploration of Rebirth Language in 1 Peter." PhD thesis, University of Toronto, Centre for the Study of Religion, 2011.

Heever, Gerhard van den. "Finding Data in Unexpected Places (Or: From Text Linguistics to Socio-rhetoric). A Socio-rhetorical Reading of John's Gospel." Pages 649–76 in vol. 2 of *Society of Biblical Literature Seminar Papers.* SBLSP 37. Atlanta: Society of Biblical Literature, 1998.

———. *From Jesus Christ to Christianity: Early Christian Literature in Context.* Pretoria: UNISA Press, 2001.

———. "'From the Pragmatics of Textures to a Christian Utopia': The Case of the Gospel of John." Pages 297–334 in *Rhetorical Criticism and the Bible.* Edited by Stanley E. Porter and Dennis L. Stamps. JSNTSup 195. Sheffield: Sheffield Academic, 2002.

Herzog II, William R. "Dissembling, a Weapon of the Weak: The Case of Christ and Caesar in Mark 12:13–17 and Romans 13:1–7." *Perspectives in Religious Studies* 2 (1994): 339–60.

"Hong Kong Ranked World's Freest Economy for Twenty-Four Consecutive Years." The Government of the Hong Kong Special Administrative Region. https://www.info.gov.hk/gia/general/201802/02/P2018020200484.htm.

Horsley, Richard. *Covenant Economics: A Biblical Vision of Justice for All*. Louisville: Westminster John Knox, 2009.

Huber, Lynn R. "Knowing Is Seeing: Theories of Metaphor Ancient, Medieval, and Modern." Pages 235–84 in *Foundations for Sociorhetorical Exploration: A Rhetoric of Religious Antiquity Reader*. Edited by Vernon K. Robbins, Robert H. von Thaden, Jr., and Bart B. Bruehler. RRA 4. Atlanta: SBL Press, 2016.

Huie-Jolly, Mary R. "Like Father, Like Son, Absolute Case, Mythic Authority: Constructing Ideology in John 5:17–23." Pages 567–95 in *Society of Biblical Literature 1997 Seminar Papers*. SBLSP 36. Atlanta: Society of Biblical Literature, 1997.

———. "The Son Enthroned in Conflict: A Socio-Rhetorical Analysis of John 5:17–23." PhD diss., University of Otago, New Zealand, 1994.

Ip, Alex Hon Ho. *A Socio-rhetorical Interpretation of the Letter to Philemon in Light of the New Institutional Economics: An Exhortation to Transform a Master-Slave Economic Relationship into a Brotherly Loving Relationship*. WUNT 2/444. Tübingen: Morh Siebeck, 2017.

Intergovernmental Panel on Climate Change. *Climate Change 2014: Synthesis Report, Contribution of Working Groups I, II and III to the Fifth Assessment Report of the Intergovernmental Panel on Climate Change*. Edited by Core Writing Team, R. K. Pachauri and L. A. Meyer. IPCC, Geneva, Switzerland.

———. *Fifth Assessment Report: Climate Change 2014*. https://www.ipcc.ch/pdf/assessment-report/ar5.

Isaak, Jon. "The Christian Community and Political Responsibility: Romans 13:1–7." *Direction* 32 (2003): 32–46.

Jasper, David. *A Short Introduction to Hermeneutics*. Louisville: Westminster John Knox, 2004.

Jeal, Roy R. "Blending Two Arts: Rhetorical Words, Rhetorical Pictures and Social Formation in the Letter to Philemon." *Sino-Christian Studies* 5 (2008): 9–38.

———. "Clothes Make the (Wo)Man." *Scriptura* 90 (2005): 685–99. Repr., pages 393–414 in *Foundations for Sociorhetorical Exploration: A Rhetoric of Religious Antiquity Reader*. Edited by Vernon K. Robbins, Robert H. von Thaden Jr., and Bart B. Bruehler. RRA 4. Atlanta: SBL Press, 2016.

———. "Emerging Christian Discourse: The Acts of Pilate as the Rhetorical Development of Devotion." *Apocrypha* 21 (2010): 151–67.

———. *Exploring Colossians: Transferred to the New Reality*. RRA. Atlanta: SBL Press, forthcoming.

———. *Exploring Philemon: Freedom, Brotherhood, and Partnership in the New Society*. RRA 2. Atlanta: SBL Press, 2015.

———. "Ideology, Argumentation and Social Direction in Romans 1." Pages 27–44 in *Human Sexuality and the Nuptial Mystery*. Edited by Roy R. Jeal. Eugene, OR: Cascade Books, 2010.

———. "Melody, Imagery and Memory in the Moral Persuasion of Paul." Pages 160–78 in *Rhetoric, Ethic and Moral Persuasion in Biblical Discourse*. Edited by Thomas H. Olbricht and Anders Eriksson. ESEC 11. New York: T&T Clark International, 2005.

———. "Rhetorical Argumentation in the Letter to the Ephesians." Pages 310–24 in *Rhetorical Argumentation in Biblical Texts: Essays from the Lund 2000 Conference*. Edited by Anders Eriksson, Thomas H. Olbricht, and Walter Übelacker. ESEC 8. Harrisburg: Trinity Press International, 2002.

———. "Sociorhetorical Intertexture." Pages 151–64 in *Exploring Intertextuality: Diverse Strategies for New Testament Interpretation of Texts*. Edited by B. J. Oropeza and Steve Moyise. Eugene, OR: Cascade Books, 2016.

———. "Starting before the Beginning: Precreation Discourse in Colossians." *Religion and Theology* 18.1–2 (2011): 287–310.

———. "Visions of Marriage in Ephesians 5." Pages 116–30 in *Human Sexuality and the Nuptial Mystery*. Edited by Roy R. Jeal. Eugene, OR: Cascade Books, 2010.

———. "Visual Exegesis: Blending Rhetorical Arts in Colossians 2:6–3:4." Pages 55–87 in *The Art of Visual Exegesis: Rhetoric; Texts; Images*. Edited by Vernon K. Robbins, Walter S. Melion, and Roy R. Jeal. ESEC 19. Atlanta: SBL Press, 2017.

Jensen, Jørgen Skafte. "Retorisk kritik: Om en ny vej I evangelieforskningen." *DTT* 55 (1992): 262–79. ET: "Rhetorical Criticism: On a New Way in Gospel Research."

Jewett, Robert. *Romans: A Commentary*. Hermeneia. Minneapolis: Fortress, 2007.

Jodamus, Johnathan. "Gendered Ideology and Power in 1 Corinthians." *JECH* 6 (2016): 1–30.

———. "An Investigation into the Construction(s) and Representation(s) of Masculinity(ies) and Femininity(ies) in 1 Corinthians." PhD diss., University of Cape Town, South Africa, 2015.

———. "Paul, the 'Real' Man: Constructions and Representations of Masculinity in 1 Corinthians." *Journal of Gender and Religion in Africa* 23 (2017): 68–94.

———. "A Socio-rhetorical Exegesis of 1 Timothy 2:8–15." MSocSci thesis, University of Cape Town, South Africa, 2005.

Kama, Bal. "Christianising Samoa's Constitution and Religious Freedom in the Pacific." DevPolicy Blog. 27 April 2017. https://tinyurl.com/SBL3814c.

Karris, Robert J., ed. *Works of St. Bonaventure: Commentary on the Gospel of Luke. Chapters 1–8*. Saint Bonaventure, NY: Franciscan Institute Publications, 2001.

Kartzow, Marianne Bjelland. *Gossip and Gender. Othering of Speech in the Pastoral Epistles*. BZNW 164. Berlin: de Gruyter, 2009.

Kennedy, George A. *New Testament Interpretation through Rhetorical Criticism*. Chapel Hill, NC: University of North Carolina Press, 1984.

———. "Reworking Aristotle's Rhetoric." Pages 77–93 in *Foundations for Sociorhetorical Exploration: A Rhetoric of Religious Antiquity Reader*. Edited by Vernon K. Robbins, Robert H. von Thaden, Jr., and Bart B. Bruehler. RRA 4. Atlanta: SBL Press, 2016.

King, Deborah. "Multiple Jeopardy, Multiple Consciousness: The Context of Black Feminist Ideology." *Signs: Journal of Women in Culture and Society* 14 (1988): 88–111.

Kingsbury, Jack D. *Matthew as Story*. 2nd edition. Philadelphia: Fortress, 1988.

———. "On Following Jesus: The 'Eager' Scribe and the 'Reluctant' Disciple (Matthew 18:18–22)." *NTS* 34 (1998): 45–59.

Kvammen, Ingeborg A. K. *Toward a Postcolonial Reading of the Epistle of James: James 2:1–13 in its Roman Imperial Context*. BINS 119. Leiden: Brill, 2013.

Lafitaga, Elekosi F. "Apocalyptic, Here and Now: The Book of Dreams (1 Enoch 83–90) and the Rhetoric of Apocalyptic Discourse in the Gospel of Matthew." PhD diss., Graduate Theological Union, Berkeley, California, 2017.

Leaupepe, Faamoana. "The Widow's Offering: A Socio-rhetorical Reading of Mark 12:41–44." Malua Theological College, Samoa, 2017.

Lee, Chul Woo. "A Socio-rhetorical Analysis of Romans 7: With Special Attention to the Law." DTh diss., University of Stellenbosch, 2001.

———. "Understanding the Law in Rom. 7:1–6: an Enthymemic Analysis." *Scriptura* 88 (2005), 126–38.

Lefebvre, Henri. *The Production of Space*. Oxford: Blackwell, 1991.

Lightstone, Jack N. *Mishnah and the Social Formation of the Early Rabbinic Guild: A Socio-rhetorical Approach*. Studies in Christianity and Judaism/Études sur le christianisme et le judaïsme 6. Waterloo: Wilfrid Laurier University Press for the Canadian Corporation for Studies in Religion/Corporation Canadienne des Sciences Réligieuses, 2002.

———. *The Rhetoric of the Babylonian Talmud: Its Social Meaning and Context*. Studies in Christianity and Judaism/Études sur le christianisme et le judaïsme 6. Waterloo: Wilfrid Laurier University Press for the Canadian Corporation for Studies in Religion/Corporation Canadienne des Sciences Réligieuses, 1994.

Lim, Sung U. "A Double-Voiced Reading of Romans 13:1–7 in Light of the Imperial Cult." *HTS Teologiese/TheologicalStudies* (*HvTSt*) 71(1) (2015): art. 2475. doi.org/10.4102/hts.v71i1.2475.

Loubser, J. A. (Bobby). "Invoking the Ancestors: Some Socio-rhetorical Aspects of the Genealogies in the Gospels of Mathew and Luke." *Neot* 39.1 (2005): 127–40.

Lykke, Nina. "Intersectional Analysis: Black Box or Useful Critical Feminist Thinking Technology?" Pages 207–20 in *Framing Intersectionality: Debates on a Multi-Faceted Concept in Gender Studies*. Edited by Helma Lutz, Maria Teresa Herrera Vivar, and Linda Supik. Burlington VT; Farnham, Surrey, UK: Ashgate, 2011.

Mack, Burton L., and Vernon K. Robbins, *Patterns of Persuasion in the Gospels*. Sonoma, CA: Polebridge Press, 1989.

Malherbe, Abraham J. *Social Aspects of Early Christianity*. 2nd ed. Philadelphia: Fortress, 1983.

Malina, Bruce J., and John J. Pilch. *Social-Science Commentary on the Letters of Paul*. Minneapolis: Fortress, 2006.

Malota, Perenise. "What Jesus Said about Divorce: A Samoan Christian Biblical

Interpretation of Matthew 19:1–9." BD thesis, Malua Theological College, Samoa, 2010.

Maier, Harry O. *Picturing Paul in Empire: Imperial Image, Text and Persuasion in Colossians, Ephesians and the Pastoral Epistles.* London: T&T Clark/Bloomsbury, 2013.

Marchal, Joseph A. *Hierarchy, Unity and Imitation: A Feminist Rhetorical Analysis of Power Dynamics in Paul's Letter to the Philippians.* Atlanta: Society of Biblical Literature, 2006.

Mathebula, Daphne. "Jonah's Attitude towards Socio-religious Change." MA thesis, Johannesburg: University of Johannesburg, 1999.

Mayhew, Susan. *A Dictionary of Geography.* Oxford: Oxford University Press, 1997.

Meeks, Wayne A. *The First Urban Christians: The Social World of the Apostle Paul.* New Haven: Yale University Press, 1983.

Meetari, Tieem. "An Interpretation of Giving Gifts in 2 Corinthians 9:1–15 from a Kiribati Perspective." BD thesis, Malua Theological College, Samoa, 2015.

Megbelayin, Olu Jerome. "A Socio-rhetorical Analysis of the Lukan Narrative of the Last Supper." PhD diss., Saint Paul University, Ottawa, 2002.

Mgaya, Gerson. *Spiritual Gifts: A Sociorhetorical Interpretation of 1 Cor 12–14.* Amazon, 2017.

Miller, Carolyn R. "The Aristotelian Topos: Hunting for Novelty." Pages 95–117 in *Foundations for Sociorhetorical Exploration: A Rhetoric of Religious Antiquity Reader.* Edited by Vernon K. Robbins, Robert H. von Thaden Jr., and Bart B. Bruehler. RRA 4. Atlanta: SBL Press, 2016.

Miller, David Jay. "Characterisations of YHWH in the Song of the Vineyard: A Multitextural Interpretation of Isaiah 5:1–7." PhD diss., University of South Africa, Pretoria, 2013.

Morrison, Toni. *Playing in the Dark: Whiteness and the Literary Imagination.* Cambridge, MA: Harvard University Press, 1992.

Moxnes, Halvor. *Putting Jesus in His Place: A Radical Vision of Household and Kingdom.* Louisville: Westminster John Knox, 2003.

Mullen, Lincoln. "The Fight to Define Romans 13." *The Atlantic.* 15 June 2018. https://tinyurl.com/SBL3814b.

Nel, Marius. "The Mysteries of the Kingdom of Heaven according to Matthew 13:10–17." *Neot* 43 (2009): 271–88.

Nofoaiga, Vaitusi. "Crowds as Jesus' Disciples in the Matthean Gospel." MTh thesis, University of Auckland, New Zealand, 2007.

———. "Exploring Discipleship in Matthew 4:12–25 from *tautuaileva* (Service/servant/serve in Between)." *Pacific Journal of Theology* 50 (2013): 61–87.

———. "Jesus the *Fiaola* (Opportunity Seeker): A Postcolonial Samoan Reading of Matthew 7:24–8:22." Pages 163–77 in *Sea of Readings: The Bible in the South Pacific.* Edited by Jione Havea. Semeia Studies 90. Atlanta: SBL Press, 2018.

———. *A Samoan Reading of Discipleship in Matthew.* IVBS 8. Atlanta: SBL Press, 2017.

———. "A Samoan Reading of Judas's Betrayal of Jesus." In *Point of View Publishing:*

Customized Course Readings. Edited by Mark Roncace and Joseph Weaver. Religion, Biblical Studies. 2018. https://tinyurl.com/SBL3814a.

North, Douglass. *Institutions, Institutional Change and Economic Performance.* Cambridge: Cambridge University Press, 1990.

———. "Transaction Cost, Institutions and Economic History." *Journal of Institutional and Theoretical Economics* 140 (1984): 7–17.

Okland, Jorunn. *Women in Their Place: Paul and the Corinthian Discourse of Gender and Sanctuary Space*. JSNTSup 269. London: T&T Clark, 2004.

Ombori, Benard N. "A Socio-rhetorical Appraisal of Jesus as Sacrifice, with Specific Reference to *Hilasterion* in Romans 3:25–26." MTh thesis, University of South Africa, Pretoria, 2013.

Oosthuizen, Martin J. "Deuteronomy 15:1–18 in Socio-rhetorical Perspective." *ZABR* 3 (1997): 64–91.

Park, Jung Sig. "The Shepherd Discourse in John 10: A Rhetorical Interpretation." DTh diss., University of Stellenbosch, 1999.

Penner, Todd, and Caroline Vander Stichele. "Unveiling Paul: Gendering Ethos in 1 Corinthians 11:2–16." Pages 214–37 in *Rhetoric, Ethic, and Moral Persuasion in Biblical Discourse: Essays from the 2002 Heidelberg Conference*. Edited by Thomas H. Olbricht and Anders Eriksson. ESEC 11. London: T&T Clark, 2005.

Phiri, Isabel Apawo. "President Frederick J. T. Chiluba of Zambia: The Christian Nation and Democracy." *Journal of Religion in Africa* 33 (2003): 401–28.

Pillay, Miranda. "Re-visioning Stigma: A Socio-rhetorical Reading of Luke 10:25–37 in the Context of HIV/AIDS in South Africa." PhD diss., University of Western Cape, South Africa, 2008.

Pinter, Dean. "Josephus and Romans 13:1–14: Providence and Imperial Power." Pages 143–50 in *Reading Romans in Context: Paul and Second Temple Judaism*. Edited by Ben C. Blackwell, John K. Goodrich, and Jason Maston. Grand Rapids: Zondervan, 2015.

Polanyi, Karl. *Great Transformation: The Political and Economic Origins of Our Time*. Boston: Beacon, 2001.

Pope Francis. *Laudato Si: On Care for our Common Home*. Vatican City: Vatican Press, 2015.

Pope John Paul II. *Centesimus Annus.* Encyclical Letter. Vatican City: Vatican Press, 1991.

"Poverty Situation," Census and Statistics Department, The Government of the Hong Kong Special Administrative Region, https://tinyurl.com/SBL3814e.

Powell, Thomas and John D. Fraser. "The Samoan Story of Creation: A 'Tala'." *The Journal of the Polynesian Society* 1,3 (1892): 164–89.

Pratt, George. *Pratt's Grammar Dictionary and Samoan Language*. Apia: Malua Printing Press, 1911.

Puaina, Seumaninoa. "Beyond Universalism: Unraveling the Anonymous Minor Characters in Matthew 15:21–28." PhD diss., Graduate Theological Union, Berkeley, California, 2016.

———. "The Feeding of the 5000 (Matthew 14:13–20): A New Missionary Paradigm for

the Congregational Church Samoa." BD thesis, Malua Theological College, Samoa, 2011.
Pupi, Challis. "A Samoan Reading of Jesus' True Family in Matthew 12:45–50." BTh thesis, Malua Theological College, Samoa, 2019.
Refiti, Albert. "Mavae and Tofiga: Spatial Exposition of the Samoan Cosmogony and Architecture." PhD diss., School of Art & Design, Auckland University of Technology, 2015.
Robinson, Peter Samuel. "A Sociorhetorical Analysis of Clark H. Pinnock's Hermeneutical Approach to Biblical Materials, with Particular Attention to the Role of Religious Experience." PhD diss., Saint Paul University, Ottawa, 2013.
Robbins, Vernon K. "Argumentative Textures in Socio-Rhetorical Interpretation." Pages 27–65 in *Rhetorical Argumentation in Biblical Texts*. Edited by Anders Eriksson, Thomas H. Olbricht, and Walter Übelacker. ESEC 8. Harrisburg, PA: Trinity Press International, 2002.
———. "Beginnings and Developments in Socio-rhetorical Interpretation." Emory University. 2004. http://tinyurl.com/SBL7103h.
———. "By Land and By Sea: A Study in Acts 13–28." *SBLSP* 15 (1976): 381–96.
———. "By Land and By Sea: The We-Passages and Ancient Sea Voyages." Pages 215–42 in *Perspectives in Luke-Acts*. Edited by Charles H. Talbert. Macon, GA: Mercer University Press; Edinburgh: T&T Clark, 1978.
———. "Conceptual Blending and Early Christian Imagination." Pages 161–95 in *Explaining Christian Origins and Early Judaism: Contributions from Cognitive and Social Science*. Edited by Petri Luomanen, Ilkka Pyysiäinen, and Risto Uro. BIS 89. Leiden: Brill, 2007. Repr., pages 329–64 in *Foundations for Sociorhetorical Exploration: A Rhetoric of Religious Antiquity Reader*. Edited by Vernon K. Robbins, Robert H. von Thaden Jr., and Bart B. Bruehler. RRA 4. Atlanta: SBL Press, 2016.
———. "The Dialectical Nature of Early Christian Discourse." *Scriptura* 59 (1996): 353–62.
———. *Exploring the Texture of Texts: A Guide to Socio-Rhetorical Interpretation*. Harrisburg, PA: Trinity Press International, 1996.
———. "From Heidelberg to Heidelberg: Rhetorical Interpretation of the Bible at the Seven 'Pepperdine' Conferences from 1992 to 2002." Pages 335–77 in *Rhetoric, Ethic and Moral Persuasion in Biblical Discourse*. Edited by Thomas H. Olbricht and Anders Eriksson. ESEC 11. New York: T&T Clark International, 2005.
———. "From the Social Sciences to Rhetography." Pages 225–44 in *Genealogies of New Testament Rhetorical Criticism*. Edited by Troy W. Martin. Minneapolis: Fortress, 2014.
———. *The Invention of Christian Discourse, Volume 1*. RRA. Dorset, UK: Deo, 2009.
———. Introduction to *Jesus the Teacher: A Socio-rhetorical Interpretation of Mark*. Philadelphia: Fortress, 1992.
———. *Jesus the Teacher: A Socio-rhetorical Interpretation of Mark*. Philadelphia: Fortress, 1984, 2009.
———. "The Present and Future of Rhetorical Analysis." Pages 33–40 in *The Rhetorical Analysis of Scripture: Essays from the 1995 London Conference*. Edited by Stanley E. Porter and Thomas H. Olbricht. JSNTSup 146. Sheffield: Sheffield Academic, 1997.

———. "Rhetography: A New Way of Seeing the Familiar Text." Pages 91–106 in *Words Well Spoken: George Kennedy's Rhetoric of the New Testament*. Edited by C. Clifton Black and Duane F. Watson. SRR 8. Waco, TX: Baylor University Press, 2008. Repr., pages 367–92 in *Foundations for Sociorhetorical Exploration: A Rhetoric of Religious Antiquity Reader*. Edited by Vernon K. Robbins, Robert H. von Thaden Jr., and Bart B. Bruehler. RRA 4. Atlanta: SBL Press, 2016.

———. "The Rhetorical Full-Turn in Biblical Interpretation: Reconfiguring Rhetorical-Political Analysis." Pages 48–60 in *Rhetorical Criticism and the Bible*. Edited by Stanley E. Porter and Dennis L. Stamps. JSNTSup 195. Sheffield: Sheffield Academic, 2002.

———. "The Rhetorical Full-Turn in Biblical Interpretation and Its Relevance for Feminist Hermeneutics." Pages 109–27 in *Her Master's Tools? Feminist and Postcolonial Engagements of Historical-Critical Discourse*. Edited by Caroline Vander Stichele and Todd Penner. GPBS 9. Atlanta: Society of Biblical Literature; Leiden: Brill, 2005.

———. *Sea Voyages and Beyond: Emerging Strategies in Socio-Rhetorical Interpretation*. ESEC 14. Atlanta: SBL Press, 2018.

———. "Socio-rhetorical Criticism: Mary, Elizabeth, and the Magnificat as a Test Case." Pages 164–209 in *The New Literary Criticism and the New Testament*. Edited by Elizabeth Struthers Malbon and Edgar V. McKnight. JSNTSup 109. Sheffield: Sheffield Academic, 1994). Repr., pages 29–74 in *Foundations for Sociorhetorical Exploration: A Rhetoric of Religious Antiquity Reader*. Edited by Vernon K. Robbins, Robert H. von Thaden Jr., and Bart B. Bruehler. RRA 4. Atlanta: SBL Press, 2016.

———. "Socio-rhetorical Criticism." Pages 311–18 in *The Oxford Encyclopedia of Biblical Interpretation*. Vol. 2. New York: Oxford University Press, 2013.

———. "Socio-rhetorical Hermeneutics and Commentary." Pages 284–97 in *EPI TO AYTO: Essays in Honour of Petr Pokorny on His Sixty-Fifth Birthday*. Edited by J. Mrazek, S. Brodsky, and R. Dvorakova. Praha-Trebenice: Mlyn Publishers, 1998.

———. "Socio-rhetorical Interpretation." Pages 192–219 in *The Blackwell Companion to The New Testament*. Edited by David E. Aune. Blackwell Companions to Religion. Chichester, UK: Wiley-Blackwell, 2010.

———. "Sociorhetorical Interpretation and the New Testament." Forthcoming in *Oxford Handbook of New Testament Rhetoric*. Edited by Mark D. Given. London: Oxford University Press, forthcoming.

———. "The Socio-rhetorical Role of Old Testament Scripture in Luke 4–19." Pages 81–93 in *Z Noveho Zakona/From the New Testament: Sbornik k narozeninam Prof. ThDr. Zdenka Sazavy*. Edited by Hana Tonzarova and Petr Melmuk, Praha: Vydala Cirkev ceskoslovenska husitska, 2001. Repr., pages 372–84 in *Sea Voyages and Beyond: Emerging Strategies in Socio-Rhetorical Interpretation*. Edited by Vernon K. Robbins. ESEC 14. Atlanta: SBL Press, 2018.

———. *The Tapestry of Early Christian Discourse: Rhetoric, Society and Ideology*. New York: Routledge, 1996.

———. "The We-Passages in Acts and Ancient Sea Voyages." *BR* 20 (1975): 5–18.

———. "Voyaging on the Sea of Life: Reflections on the We-Passages in Acts." *BR* 65 (2020): 58–76.

———. "Why Participate in African Biblical Interpretation?" Pages 275–91 in *Interpreting the New Testament in Africa*. Edited by Mary N. Getui, Tinyiko S. Maluleke, and Justin Ukpong. Nairobi, Kenya: Acton Publishers, 2001.

Robbins, Vernon K., Robert H. von Thaden Jr., and Bart B. Bruehler, eds. *Foundations for Sociorhetorical Exploration: A Rhetoric of Religious Antiquity Reader*. RRA 4. Atlanta: SBL Press, 2016.

Romero, Mary. *Introducing Intersectionality*. Malden, MA: Polity Press, 2018.

Rostovtzeff, Michael. *The Social and Economic History of the Roman Empire*. Oxford: Clarendon, 1988.

Sack, Robert. *Human Territoriality: In Theory and History*. Cambridge: Cambridge University Press, 1986

Samuelu, Caesar. "Head Covering for Women in 1 Corinthians 11:2–16." BD thesis, Malua Theological College, Samoa, 2008.

Schüssler Fiorenza, Elisabeth. "Challenging the Rhetorical Half-Turn: Feminist and Rhetorical Biblical Criticism." Pages 28–53 in *Rhetoric, Scripture and Theology: Essays from the 1994 Pretoria Conference*. Edited by Stanley E. Porter and Thomas H. Olbricht. JSNTSup 131. Sheffield: Sheffield Academic, 1996.

———. "Disciplinary Matters: A Critical Rhetoric and Ethic of Inquiry." Pages 9–32 in *Rhetoric, Ethic, and Moral Persuasion in Biblical Discourse: Essays from the 2002 Heidelberg Conference*. Edited by Thomas H. Olbricht and Anders Eriksson. ESEC 11. London: T&T Clark, 2005.

———. "The Ethics of Interpretation: De-Centering Biblical Scholarship." *JBL* 107 (1988): 3–17.

Seb, George P. "A Socio-rhetorical Analysis of YHWH's Speeches in Selected Texts of Exodus 2–11 with Focus on Redemption and the Knowledge of YHWH." DTh diss., United Theological College, Bangalore, India, forthcoming.

Segovia, Fernando F. "And They Began to Speak in Other Tongues: Competing Modes of Discourse in Contemporary Biblical Criticism." Pages 1–34 in *Reading from This Place: Social Location and Biblical Interpretation in the United States*. Edited by Fernando F. Segovia and Mary Ann Tolbert. Vol. 1. Minneapolis: Fortress, 1995.

———. *Decolonizing Biblical Studies: A View from the Margins*. New York: Orbis, 2000.

———. "Liberation Hermeneutics: Revisiting the Foundations in Latin America." Pages 106–32 in *Toward a New Heaven and a New Earth: Essays in Honor of Elisabeth Schüssler Fiorenza*. Edited by Fernando F. Segovia. Maryknoll: Orbis, 2003.

Setu, Leuelu. "Revisiting Judas's Betrayal of Jesus in the Gospel of Matthew 26:14–16, 47–45; 27:3–10." BD with Honor thesis, Malua Theological College, Samoa, 2018.

Shaaber, Vincilo G. "Revisiting the Addressees of the Apocalypse: A Socio-rhetorical Reading of Revelation 13." MTh thesis, United Theological College, Bangalore, India, forthcoming.

Siahaan, Rospita Deliana. "Speaking in Tongues in Public Worship? A Socio-rhetorical Approach to 1 Corinthians 12–14." PhD diss., Lutheran Theological Seminary, Shatin, Hong Kong, 2015. Published in Indonesian translation as *Bahasa Roh Dalam Ibadah Jemaat? Tafsir Sosio-Retorika 1 Korintus 12–14*. Jakarta: BPK-GM, 2017.

Singgih, Emanuel Gerrit. "Towards a Post Colonial Interpretation of Romans 13:1–7: Karl Barth, Robert Jewett and the Context of Reformation in Present-Day Indonesia." *Asia Journal of Theology* 23 (2009): 111–22.
Soja, Edward W. *Thirdspace: Journeys to Los Angeles and Other Real-and-Imagined Places.* Oxford: Blackwell, 1996.
Stein, Robert H. "The Argument of Romans 13:1–7." *NovT* 31 (1989): 325–43.
Stenström, Hanna. "Historical-Critical Approaches and the Emancipation of Women: Unfulfilled Promises and Remaining Possibilities." Pages 31–46 in *Her Master's Tools? Feminist and Postcolonial Engagements of Historical-Critical Discourse.* Edited by Caroline Vander Stichele and Todd Penner. Atlanta: Society of Biblical Literature, 2005.
Stowers, Clarke. "Names as Hermeneutics to Read Texts: *Fofogaolevai* and John the Baptizer (Mark 1:1–15)." BTh thesis, Malua Theological College, Samoa, 2017.
Subramani, N. "Imagery of Love as a Paradigm for Covenantal Relationship in the Book of Hosea: A Socio-Rhetorical Reading." DTh diss., South Asia Theological Research Institute, Union Biblical Seminary, Pune, Maharashtra, India, 2018.
Sugirtharajah, R. S., ed. *Vernacular Hermeneutics.* Cambridge: Cambridge University Press, 2009.
Tan, Kimseng. *The Rhetoric of Abraham's Faith in Romans 4.* ESEC 20. Atlanta: SBL Press, 2018.
Tapelu, Timoteo. "*Tautua* as a Hermeneutical Tool to Understand Paul's View of Justification by Faith in 2 Corinthians 9:6–15 and the EFKS Ministry." BD thesis, Malua Theological College, Samoa, 2016.
Tate, W. Randolph. "Socio-rhetorical Criticism." Pages 342–46 in *Interpreting the Bible: A Handbook of Terms and Methods.* Peabody, MA: Hendrickson, 2006.
Tavalani, Kuresa. "Jesus' Encounter with the Samaritan Woman (John 4:16–30) from *Tuagane* (Brother to a Sister) Perspective." BTh thesis, Malua Theological College, Samoa, 2016.
Taylor, Charles. *Philosophy and the Human Sciences: Philosophical Papers.* Cambridge: Cambridge University Press, 1985.
Thaden, Robert H. von, Jr. "A Cognitive Turn: Conceptual Blending within a Sociorhetorical Framework." Pages 285–328 in *Foundations for Sociorhetorical Exploration: A Rhetoric of Religious Antiquity Reader.* Edited by Vernon K. Robbins, Robert H. von Thaden Jr., and Bart B. Bruehler. RRA 4. Atlanta: SBL Press, 2016.
———. *Sex, Christ, and Embodied Cognition: Paul's Wisdom for Corinth.* ESEC 16. Atlanta: SBL Press, 2017.
Theissen, Gerd. *The First Followers of Jesus: A Sociological Analysis of the Earliest Christianity.* Translated by John Bowden. London: SCM, 1978.
———. *Gospel Writing and Church Politics: A Socio-rhetorical Approach.* Chuen King Lecture Series 3. Hong Kong: Theology Division, Chung Chi College, Chinese University of Hong Kong, 2001.
Tokaia, Kaititi. "A Kiribati Reading of the Wedding Feast in Matthew 22:1–14." BD thesis with Honors, Malua Theological College, Samoa, 2019.

Trainor, Michael. *About Earth's Child: An Ecological Listening to the Gospel of Luke.* Earth Bible Commentary 2. Sheffield: Sheffield Phoenix, 2012.

———. *Voices from the Edge: Luke's Gospel in Our World.* North Blackburn, Australia: Collins Dove, 1991.

Tumutalie, Faalefu. "Re-reading Matthew 22:15–22 Amid a Taxation Law Affecting Church Ministers in Samoa." BTh thesis, Malua Theological College, Samoa, 2018.

Tupparainen, R. P. "The Role(s) of the Spirit-Paraclete in John 16:4b–15. A Socio-rhetorical Investigation." PhD Diss., University of South Africa, Pretoria, 2007.

Vander Stichele, Caroline and Todd Penner. "Mastering the Tools or Retooling the Masters? The Legacy of Historical-Critical Discourse." Pages 1–30 in *Her Masters Tools? Feminist and Postcolonial Engagements of Historical-Critical Discourse.* Edited by Caroline Vander Stichele and Todd Penner. Atlanta: Society of Biblical Literature, 2005.

Varghese, Santosh V. "Woe-Oracles in Habakkuk 2:6–20: A Socio-rhetorical Reading." MTh thesis, Faith Theological Seminary, Manakala, Kerala, India, 2009.

Vasquez, Victor Manuel Morales. *Contours of Biblical Reception Theory: Studies in the Rezeptionsgeschichte of Romans 13.1–7.* Göttingen: V&R Unipress, 2012.

Vatanitawake, Isoa Cailala. "*Tuirara,* The Standing One: A Sociorhetorical Reading of Acts 6:1–7 in the Context of *Tuirara—Talatala* Relationship in the Methodist Church in Fiji." MTh thesis, Pacific Theological College, Suva, Fiji, 2019.

Vonck, Pol. "All Authority Comes from God: Romans 13:1–7: A Tricky Text About Obedience to Political Power." *African Ecclesial Review* 26 (1984): 338–47.

Waal, Kayle B. de. *A Socio-rhetorical Interpretation of the Seven Trumpets of Revelation: The Apocalyptic Challenge to Earthly Empire.* Lewiston, NY: Edwin Mellen, 2012.

Wainwright, Elaine M. "Feminist Criticism and the Gospel of Matthew." Pages 83–117 in *Methods for Matthew.* Edited by Mark Allan Powell. Cambridge: Cambridge University Press, 2009.

———. *Habitat, Human, and Holy: An Eco-rhetorical Reading of the Gospel of Matthew.* EBC 6. Sheffield: Sheffield Phoenix, 2016.

———. "Reading Matthew 3–4: Jesus—Sage, Seer, Sophia, Son of God." *JSNT* 77 (2000): 25–43.

Wan, Sze-Kar. "Coded Resistance: Rereading Romans 13:1–7." Pages 173–84 in *The Bible in the Public Square: Reading the Signs of the Times.* Edited by Cynthia Briggs Kittredge, Ellen Bradshaw Aitken, and Jonathan A. Draper. Minneapolis: Fortress, 2008.

Wanamaker, Charles A. "'By the Power of God': Rhetoric and Ideology in 2 Corinthians 10–13." Pages 194–221 in *Fabrics of Discourse: Essays in Honor of Vernon K. Robbins.* Edited by David B. Gowler, L Gregory Bloomquist, and Duane F. Watson. New York: Trinity Press International, 2003.

———. "The Power of the Absent Father: A Socio-Rhetorical Analysis of 1 Corinthians 4:14–5:13." Pages 339–64 in *The New Testament Interpreted: Essays in Honour of Bernard C. Lategan.* Edited by Cilliers Breytenbach, Johan C. Thom, and Jeremy Punt. Leiden: Brill, 2006.

———. "A Rhetoric of Power: Ideology and 1 Corinthians 1–4. Pages 115–37 in *Paul and the Corinthians: Studies on a Community in Conflict. Essays in Honour of Margaret Thrall*. Edited by Trevor J. Burke and J. Keith Elliott. NovTSup 109. Leiden: Brill, 2003.
Watson, Duane F. "Vernon Robbins' Socio-rhetorical Criticism: a Review." JSNT 70 (1998): 67–115.
———. "Why We Need Socio-rhetorical Commentary and What It Might Look Like." Pages 129–57 in *Rhetorical Criticism and the Bible*. Edited by Stanley E. Porter and Dennis L. Stamps. JSNTSup 195. Sheffield: Sheffield Academic, 2002.
Webster, Alexander F. C. "St. Paul's Political Advice to the Haughty Gentile Christians in Rome: An Exegesis of Romans 13:1–7." *St Vladimir's Theological Quarterly* 25 (1981): 259–82.
Wenkel, David H. *Joy in Luke-Acts: The Intersection of Rhetoric, Narrative, and Emotion*. Paternoster Biblical Monographs Series. Crownhill, UK: Paternoster, 2015.
Wiefel, Wolfgang. "The Jewish Community in Ancient Rome and the Origins of Roman Christians (Revised and Expanded)." Pages 85–101 in *The Romans Debate*. Edited by Karl P. Donfried. Peabody, MA: Hendrickson Publishers, 1991.
Wong, Michelle. "Why the Wealth Gap? Hong Kong's Disparity between Rich and Poor is Greatest in Forty-Five Years, So What Can be Done?" South China Morning Press https://www.scmp.com/news/hong-kong/society/article/2165872/why-wealth-gap-hong-kongs-disparity-between-rich-and-poor.
Wyeth, Grant. "Samoa Officially Becomes a Christian State: The Constitutional Change Is Aimed at Avoiding Religious Unrest." *The Diplomat*. 16 June 2017.
Wilson, Bryan R. *Magic and the Millennium: A Sociological Study of Religious Movements of Protest among Tribal and Third-World Peoples*. New York: Harper & Row, 1973.
Wuellner, Wilhelm. "Hermeneutics and Rhetorics: From 'Truth and Method' to 'Truth and Power'." *Scriptura* 3 (1989): 1–54.
Yeo, Khiok-khng. "Introduction: Navigating Romans through Cultures." Pages 1–28 in *Navigating Romans through Cultures: Challenging Readings by Charting a New Course*. Edited by Yeo Khiok–khng. New York: T&T Clark International, 2004.
Yuval-Davis, Nira. "Beyond the Recognition and Re-distribution Dichotomy: Intersectionality and Stratification." Pages 155–69 in *Framing Intersectionality: Debates on a Multi-Faceted Concept in Gender Studies*. Edited by Helma Lutz, Maria Teresa Herrera Vivar, and Linda Supik. Burlington, VT; Farnham, Surrey UK: Ashgate, 2011.

Contributors

Fatilua Fatilua is Lecturer of New Testament and Hellenistic Greek in the Department of Biblical Studies, Pacific Theological College, Suva, Fiji.

Alex Hon Ho Ip is Assistant Professor of Divinity School of Chung Chi, Chinese University of Hong Kong, Hong Kong.

Roy R. Jeal is Professor of Religion at Booth University College in Winnipeg, Manitoba, Canada.

Johnathan Jodamus is Senior Lecturer of New Testament and Gender Studies at the University of the Western Cape, Cape Town, South Africa.

Vaitusi Nofoaiga is Vice Principal and Head of New Testament Studies at Malua Theological College in Malua, Samoa.

Vernon K. Robbins is Professor Emeritus of Religion-Winship Distinguished Research Professor in the Humanities, Emory University in Atlanta, Georgia.

Shively T. J. Smith is Assistant Professor of New Testament at Boston University School of Theology in Boston, Massachusetts.

Michael Trainor is Senior Lecturer in Biblical Studies at the Australian Catholic University, Adelaide Campus, South Australia.

Duane F. Watson is Professor Emeritus of New Testament Studies at Malone University in Canton, Ohio.

Ancient Sources Index

Hebrew Bible

Exodus
2–11 28

Deuteronomy 28
15:1–18 22

1 Kings
5–8 53
6:14–18 53
6:29 53
6:36 53
7:15 53
7:15–22 53
7:19 53
7:21 53
7:23–26 53
7:39 53
7:44 53

2 Chronicles
3:15 53

Psalms
23 24

Isaiah
5:1–7 23

Hosea 28

Habakkuk
2:6–20 28

Deuterocanonical Books

Judith 96

Sirach 52
18:7 6
38:24–39:11 25
44–50 53

New Testament

Matthew 23, 29, 30, 48, 58, 59, 61
3–4 .... 60, 75
4:12–25 29
4:18–25 58
7:24–8:22 29
8:5–13 28
8:21–22 58
12:45–50 30
13:10–17 23
14:13–20 29
15:21–28 29
18:18–22 58

19:1–9	29	Romans	
22:1–14	30	1	24, 27, 34
22:15–22	30	3:25–26	23
23	22	4	23
26:14–16	30	7	22
26:45–47	30	7:1–6	22
27:3–10	30	12–15	84
		12:2	77, 78
Mark	26, 28	12:19	77
1:1–15	30	13:1–7	4, 5, 29, 71–86
5:1–20	28	13:4	78
7:24–30	30	13:5	77
12:13-17	76	13:8–14	76
12:41–44	30	14:1	77
Luke	23, 24, 25, 27, 29	1 Corinthians	23, 94, 97
1–8	47	1–4	97
1:26–56	13	4:14–5:13	97
4–19	21	6:1–11	29
8:24	47	8:1–3	6
10:25–37	3, 23, 39, 40	11:2–16	29, 99
14	24	12–14	28
14:1–24	20, 22		
18	26	2 Corinthians	
18:35–19:48	52, 54	9:1–15	29
19:1–10	54	9:6–15	30
19:3–4	55	10–13	23, 97
19:4	53–55		
19:5	55	Galatians	108
19:7	54		
21	24	Ephesians	26, 27
		5	27
John	23, 25		
4:16–30	30	Philippians	25, 92
5:17–23	21		
10	22	Colossians	26, 27, 28
16:4b–15	23	2:6–3:4	27
Acts	24, 25, 27	1 Timothy	26, 27
6:1–7	30	2:18–25	23, 90
9:1–30	21		
13–28	11	2 Timothy	26, 27
17:15–18:1	26		

Titus	26, 27
Philemon	27, 28, 107
James	27
1 Peter	26
Revelation	28
13	28

Other Ancient Texts

| Acts of Pilate | 27 |

1 Enoch
| 83–90 | 30 |

Origen, *Commentary on Gospel of John*
| XIII.3–42 (John 4:13–15) | 25 |

Sibylline Oracles
| 1–2 | 25 |

Modern Authors Index

Abraham, Christina 26
Afioga, Latu 30 n. 48
Aiono, Fanaafi Le Tagaloa 73 nn. 12–14, 82 n. 57
Antonyraj, Sebastian Victor 28 n. 39
Ao, Chubamongba 28 n. 39
Asumang, Annang 23–24 n. 23
Bailey, Jon Nelson 86
Barclay, John 108 n. 17
Barton, Stephen 58 n. 1
Beech, Timothy 25 n. 28
Berquist, Jon L. 3, 37, 51–52
Bertschmann, Helene Dorothea 79 n. 41
Betz, Hans Dieter 12
Beyrouti, François 25 n. 28
Bhabha, Homi K. 74 n. 18
Blanton, Thomas R. IV 101 n. 2
Bloomquist, L. Gregory 2, 20, 24–26, 34–35, 38, 40
Boer, Roland 80, 84
Bonneau, Normand 26
Botha, Jan 75 nn. 25–26, 78 n. 38–39, 81 n. 53
Boyer, Susan 75, 77
Braun, Willi 20–21, 24 n. 25
Bruehler, Bart B. 3–4, 34–36, 38–39, 52 n. 17, 53–55, 109 n. 20
Camp, Claudia V. 3, 52–53
Canavan, Rosemary 28 n. 42
Carney, T. F. 15
Collins, Patricia Hill 91–92, 96 n. 25
Combrink, H. J. Bernard 19, 22, 30
Corlett-MacDonald, Nina 28 n. 42
Crenshaw, Kimberlé W. 91, 95
Czachesz, István 21
Draper, Jonathan A. 71 n. 1
Dreyfus, Hubert L. 98
Dube, Musa W. 96
Dunn, James D. G. 76, 77 n.33, 84
Dyck, Harold J. 80 n. 52
Dyson, Michael Eric 33 n. 2
Eilperin, Juliet 56 n. 1
Fatilua, Fatilua 4, 29 n. 47, 71
Fauconnier, Gilles 14 n. 17, 16
Feagaimaalii-Luamanu, Joyetter 72 n. 4
Feinberg, Paul D. 76
Fernandez, Cyprian E. 21 n. 39
Finbow, Douglas 25, n. 28
Finley, Moses 105
Fitzmyer, Joseph A. 76 n. 27, 83
Fraser, John D. 73 n. 11
Fung, Ben 25 n. 28
Gadamer, Hans-Georg 59, 64
Gager, John G. 39
Geisterfer, Priscilla 26, 89, n. 2

Gowler, David B.   19, 30, n. 6
Groenewegen, John   106 nn. 12–13
Gruca-Macaulay, Alexandra   25 n. 28
Gunn, Têtê Délali (Éloi)   26
Habel, Norman C.   48 n. 5
Hammer, Keir   26 n. 34
Heever, Gerhard van den   23
Herzog II, William R.   76 n. 28
Horsley, Richard   101 n. 2
Huber, Lynn R.   37, 109 n.18
Huie-Jolly, Mary R.   21
Ip, Alex Hon Ho   1, 5, 28 n. 40, 101, 107 n. 14
Isaak, Jon   78
Jeal, Roy R.   1, 2, 25 n. 27, 26, 27 nn. 35–37
Jensen, Jørgen Skafte   20
Jewett, Robert   78 n. 37, 89 n. 44
Jodamus, Johnathan   5, 23 n. 21, 89, 90 n. 3, 91 n. 4, 94 n. 16, 97 n. 30
Kama, Bal   71 n. 3
Karris, Robert J.   57 n. 4
Kartzow, Marianne Bjelland   27 n. 38
Kennedy, George A.   1, 12, 64–65, 67–68, 109
King, Deborah   91 n. 7
Kingsbury, Jack D.   58 nn. 1–2
Kvammen, Ingeborg A. K.   27 n. 38
Lafitaga, Elekosi F.   30
Leaupepe, Faamoana   30 n. 48
Lee, Chul Woo   22. n. 18
Lefebvre, Henri   15, 52
Lightstone, Jack N.   17 n. 24
Lim, Sung U.   83, 84 n. 66
Loubser, J. A. (Bobby)   23 n. 23
Lykke, Nina   95 n. 21
Mack, Burton L.   12
Maier, Harry O.   26 n. 34
Malherbe, Abraham J.   12
Malina, Bruce J.   76 n. 32
Malota, Perenise   29

Marchal, Joseph A.   92
Mathebula, Daphne   22
Mayhew, Susan   66 n. 24
Meeks, Wayne A.   12, 36, 95
Meetari, Tieem   29 n. 48
Megbelayin, Olu Jerome   26
Mgaya, Gerson   28
Miller, Carolyn R.   64–67
Miller, David Jay   23 n. 20
Morrison, Toni   33–35, 41
Moxnes, Halvor   58 n. 3
Mullen, Lincoln   71 n. 1
Nel, Marius   23 n 18
Nofoaiga, Vaitusi   2, 4, 28–29, 57, 61 n. 13, 72 n. 7, 74, 81 n. 57
North, Douglass   5, 105–06
Økland, Jorunn   99 n. 39
Ombori, Benard N.   23 n. 20
Oosthuizen, Martin J.   22
Park, Jung Sig   22 n. 18
Penner, Todd   26 n. 32, 89 n. 2, 98 n. 32, 99 n. 36
Phiri, Isabel Apawo   71 n. 1
Pickett, Raymond   101 n. 2
Pilch, John J.   76 n. 32
Pillay, Miranda   3, 23, 39, 40
Pinter, Dean   84, 85 n. 69
Polanyi, Karl   5, 105
Pope Francis   56
Pope John Paul II   56
Powell, Thomas   73 n. 11
Pratt, George   72 n. 8, 73 n. 10, 81 n. 54
Puaina, Seumaninoa   29
Pupi, Challis   30 n. 48
Rabinow, Paul   98
Refiti, Albert   73 nn. 11–12
Robinson, Peter Samuel   25 n. 28
Robbins, Vernon K.   1–3, 5, 11–17, 19–27, 33 n. 3, 34, 36, 38, 39 n. 22, 48–49, 50 n. 8, 55, 60–69, 75 n. 21, 79 n. 48, 89, 90 n. 2, 92 n. 11, 93–94, 95 n. 19, 96–99, 109

Robbins, Vernon K., Robert H. von Thaden Jr., and Bart B. Bruehler 1 n. 1, 13 n. 11, 15 n 18, 16 n. 20, 19 n. 2, 24 n. 26, 27 n. 36, 33 n. 3, 34 n. 6, 35 nn. 8–9, 37 nn. 14–15, 39 n. 20, 50 n. 7, 52 n. 16, 93 n. 14, 94 n. 13, 109 nn. 18, 20
Romero, Mary 91 n. 5, 92 n. 8
Rostovtzeff, Michael 5, 105
Sack, Robert 15, 53–54
Samuelu, Caesar 29
Schüssler Fiorenza, Elisabeth 13, 26, 36, 63, 89–90, 92, 96–97, 99 n. 36
Seb, George P. 28 n. 39
Segovia, Fernando F. 58, 59 nn. 4, 6, 96 n. 23, 99 n. 36
Setu, Leuelu 30 n. 48
Shaaber, Vincilo G. 28 n. 39
Siahaan, Rospita Deliana 28 n. 40
Singgih, Emanuel Gerrit 77 n. 36
Soja, Edward W. 15, 37
Spithoven, Antoon 106 nn. 12–13
Stein, Robert H. 75 n. 23, 79 n. 45
Stenström, Hanna 99 n. 36
Stowers, Clarke 30 n. 48
Subramani, N. 28 n. 39
Sugirtharajah, R. S. 59 n. 6, 80 n. 51
Tan, Kimseng 23 n. 21
Tapelu, Timoteo 30 n. 48
Tate, W. Randolph 20 n. 5
Tavalani, Kuresa 30 n. 48
Taylor, Charles 65
Thaden, Robert H. von, Jr. 37, 68, 94
Theissen, Gerd 27, 28 n. 2
Tokaia, Kaititi 30 n. 48
Trainor, Michael 1, 3–4, 7, 45
Trudinger, Peter 48 n. 5
Tumutalie, Faalefu 30 n. 48
Tupparainen, R. P. 23 n. 20

Turner, Mark 14 n. 17, 16
Van Den Berg, Annette 106 nn. 12–13
Vander Stichele, Caroline 26 n. 32, 89 n. 2, 98 n. 32, 99 n. 36
Varghese, Santosh V. 28 n. 39
Vasquez, Victor Manuel Morales 83 n. 59
Vatanitawake, Isoa Cailala 30 n. 48
Vonck, Pol 79 n. 42
Waal, Kayle B. De 28 n. 42
Wainwright, Elaine M. 2–3, 28, 48–51, 59 n. 5, 70 n. 10, 75 n. 22
Wan, Sze-Kar 77 n. 34, 90
Wanamaker, Charles A. 23, 97 n. 30
Watson, Duane F. 1–2, 11, 15 n. 18, 19, 22 n. 17, 23 n. 21, 24 n. 26, 25 n. 27, 97 n. 30
Webster, Alexander F. C. 76 n. 29, 82 n. 58
Wenkel, David H., 27 n. 38
Wiefel, Wolfgang 83
Wong, Michelle 102 n. 3
Wyeth, Grant 71 n. 2
Wilson, Bryan R. 12, 13 n. 8
Wuellner, Wilhelm 13, 36
Yeo, Khiok–khng 80
Yuval-Davis, Nira 95 n. 22

Subject Index

aesthetic theory (Gadamer), 59
Africa, 5, 24
ambiguity, ambiguities, 82–84
anamnesis, 47, 48–51, 52, 53, 55, 56
anthropocentricism, 56
anthropological resources, 3, 38, 39, 61, 63
Aristotle, 37, 64, 67
    Aristotle's view of perception and image, 64–65
    Aristotelian topoi, 66–67
Australia, 3, 28, 31, 45–46
Ben Sira, 52–53
Bible, 47–48, 57–59, 62, 65–69
Bible in the Pacific, 72
Bonn, 22
Canada, 2, 20, 26, 31
Cape Town, 23
Christianity and western influence, 36, 74
Christianity in the Pacific, 72
church-state relations, 71, 81–86
chreia, 12
class, 5, 61, 80, 90, 93, 97
classical rhetoric, 6, 11, 15, 67–68
climate change, 3, 45–50
cognitive sciences, 11, 14, 16, 25, 36, 37, 64
cognitive turn, 4, 68

conceptual blending, 4, 6, 14–17, 67–68, 90–94, 109
conceptual integration theory, 68
connections, 4, 72–74, 79, 81–82, 85
contextual conversations, 39
covenant, 47, 81
criticism, 20–22, 36, 37, 39, 58–60, 63, 92, 98, 99
cultural geography, 6, 15–16, 51
culture, 3, 6, 13, 15, 29, 36, 37, 50–51, 54, 62, 65–66, 72, 73–74, 85
Czech Republic, 2, 21
Denmark, 2
diaspora, 85
discipleship, 4, 58, 61–62, 74
discovery in rhetoric, 6, 65, 67, 69
diversity, 17, 35–36, 103–05
Durham, 22
economics, 5, 101–11
eco-theology, 3–4, 47–66
embedded economy, 5, 105, 109–10
embodied epistemology, 92, 97, 100
enthymeme, 14–15
environment, 33, 38, 40, 45–56, 66, 71, 84, 86
ethos, 67, 109
faia analysis, 71–86
feminist, 21, 26, 59, 92, 96–98

feminist rhetorical interpretation, 2
Fiji, 2, 20, 31
Finland, 2, 28
firstspace, 3, 52–53
formal institution, 102–10
gender, 5, 89–100
gender-critical, 5, 89–100
gospel, gospels, 4, 12, 21, 25, 29–30, 40 47, 53–55, 58, 61–62, 64, 69
Göteborg, 2, 22
governing authorities, 72, 75–82
Great Barrier Reef, 3, 45–46, 56
hermeneutics, 4, 24, 36, 40, 55–56, 60–62, 64, 85, 106
   biblical hermeneutics, 47–51
   classical hermeneutics, 59
   hermeneutic of *fiaola* (opportunity seeker), 4, 61
   hermeneutic of *tautuaileva* (serve in-between spaces), 4, 61, 74
   hermeneutical conundrum, 40
Hong Kong, 1, 2, 5, 27–28, 102–04
Hungary, 21
Iceland, 30–31
identity, 54, 60, 65–66, 80, 91, 93, 95, 99
ideology, 36
India, 2, 28, 40
indigenous, 21
Indonesia, 28, 31, 40
informal institution, 102–10
institutional environment, 108
interpretive analytics, 5–6, 92, 95–98, 104
interpretive environment, 38
intersectionality, 5, 7, 89–100
interpretive analytics, 5–7, 11, 34–38, 40, 50, 60, 69, 90, 92–93, 95–96, 98, 104, 107
Johannesburg, 22
Maori, 21

metaphor, 37, 67, 91, 97, 107, 109, 110
methodological hegemony, 35, 38, 55
modes of discourse, 6, 14–17, 37, 39, 50, 109
Nebraska, 30
neo-Aristotelian theory of invention, 67
neoclassical, 2
New Institutional Economics (NIE), 3, 5, 101–2, 104–10
New Zealand, 20
Nigeria, 26
Norway, 2, 30, 31
Oceania, 2–4, 64, 68–69
Otago, 21
Ottawa, 2, 24, 25, 26
Paul, 5, 26, 27, 35, 40, 72, 75, 79–81, 83–84, 91, 94, 99, 108
pathos, 67, 109
Pepperdine Conferences, 2, 24, 27, 89
place, 4, 15–16, 50, 52, 53–54, 58, 65–67
plurality of strategies, 38
politics, 5, 7, 36, 60, 64, 71, 74, 80–82, 84, 86, 90, 92, 97
Port Elizabeth, 22
power, 5, 14, 17, 33, 61, 84, 92–93, 95, 97, 98
Prague, 21
Pretoria, 2, 22–24, 30, 89
progymnasmata, 12
race, 5, 90, 91–93, 97
radical rhetoric, 4, 68, 109
relations, 5, 54, 69, 72–76, 77–79, 80–85, 95, 98, 102–9
rhetography, 4, 15–17, 25, 27, 50, 65, 67–69, 93–95, 104, 108–10
rhetology, 15–17, 67–68, 93–95
rhetorical invention, 33, 66–78
rhetorolects, 14–17, 27, 50, 93–94,

104, 108–10
Romans, Letter to the, 35, 71–86
Samoa, Samoan, 2, 4, 7, 20, 21, 29, 31, 57–69, 71–86
  Samoan Constitution, 71
  Samoan context, 7, 29, 57–69, 72, 74
  Samoan identity, 66
  Samoan reading, 63, 66, 72
self-conscious approach, 4, 63–64
Scotland, 30
secondspace, 52
slavery, Roman, 106
sociological resources, 3, 38–39, 61, 63
Sociorhetorical Interpretation (SRI)
  definition, 3, 11, 35—39, 48–51, 57–63
  emergence of, 1–3, 11–41, 63, 98
  international emergence, 1–3, 19–31
  sociorhetorical analytic, 5–7, 11, 34–38, 39, 50, 60, 69, 92–98, 104
  SRI and boundaries of rhetorical analysis, 64
  sociorhetorical model of textual communication, 3, 49, 61–62, 69
  Robbins's sociorhetorical approach, 11, 49, 57–63, 67–69
South Africa, 2, 3, 5, 20, 22–23, 30, 39–40, 71, 89–90, 97–99
space, 4, 15–16, 37, 39, 51–56, 61, 65, 66–67, 72–75, 80, 83–86
spatiality, 51, 64
  critical spatiality, 3, 6, 16, 51–55, 94
  critical spatiality theory, 15–16
special rhetoric of place, 4, 66

speech (logos) in texts, 67–69, 108–10
Sweden, 2, 22
sycamore tree, 4, 53–55
Tanzania, 28
Tel Aviv, 22
Temple, 3, 11, 15, 52–53
textures, 3, 4–7, 13–14, 17, 19, 36, 37, 48, 64, 93–94, 104
  argumentative texture, 13, 78–79, 94
  ecological texture, 3, 48
  economic texture, 5, 102, 107–10
  ideological texture, 5, 13, 17, 35, 49–50, 92, 107
  inner textures, 13, 17, 35, 49–50, 75–77
  intersectional texture, 5, 7, 89–100
  intertexture, 12, 13, 35, 49, 50–51
  narrational texture, 26
  progressive texture, 13, 77
  religious textures, 7
  sacred texture, 13–14, 35, 50
  social and cultural texture, 3, 12, 13, 17, 35, 49, 50–51, 79–81, 107
Togo, 26
theology, 22, 84
thirdspace, 4, 52–53
topos, topoi, 4, 6, 25, 37, 64–67, 109
traditional methods of interpretation, 58–60
United States, 2, 20, 71, 74, 102
visual imagery, 4, 6, 16, 64, 67
worldly rhetoric in NT texts, 68, 109, 110
Zacchaeus, 4, 54–55

www.ingramcontent.com/pod-product-compliance
Lightning Source LLC
Chambersburg PA
CBHW031403230426
43670CB00006B/625